Essential Guide to Exotic Pets

Beginner's Handbook to Choose, Care for, and Handle with Confidence

Luna Wildheart

HW Premier Publishing LLC

Contents

Introduction

Welcome to the Wild Side

I t all started one quiet afternoon when I wandered into a tucked-away pet shop nestled in a sleepy part of the city. The lights were low;the air was still, and the walls seemed to hum with quiet secrets. In that mysterious little store, I met Trevor—a tiny chameleon with a big personality.I watched, fascinated, as he melted into a plastic fern like it was second nature. In that moment, I realized that owning an exotic pet isn't just about food or upkeep—it's about entering a world where the unexpected is just part of the daily routine.

This book is for anyone who's captivated by these remarkable creatures. It's designed to equip you—the aspiring exotic pet owner—with the practical knowledge and confidence to care for your new companion the right way. Think of it as your down-to-earth guide through the sometimes confusing,always fascinating world of exotic pet care. Whether you're trying to outsmart runaway gecko or figure out why your snake loves hiding in your sneakers, you'll find real-world advice here.

A bit about me: My adventure with exotic pets began with a curious iguana named Spike. What started as a hobby quickly turned into a deep and lasting passion. Over the years, I've thrown myself into learning all I can about these animals and sharing what I've discovered with others who are just as curious. My mission? To give you clear, practical help so you can enjoy the rewards—and meet the responsibilities—of being an exotic pet owner.

Inside this book, you'll find everything from how to create the ideal habitat and what to feed your pet, to how to keep them healthy and navigate legal regulations (yep, even ones about tarantulas crossing state lines). Each chapter offers tips tailored to specific species, making it simple to give your unique little companion exactly what they need.

What sets this book apart? It's not just a textbook. You'll find interactive features, visual guides, and easy-to-follow breakdowns of what each species needs. We've even included checklists to keep you organized and links to online resources for when you're asking yourself, "Wait, is my parrot supposed to do that?"

I get it—this world can be overwhelming. There's a lot to learn and a lot to get right. That's why I've made this book straightforward,approachable, and free of unnecessary jargon. Just honest, useful advice to help you succeed.

Above all, ethical care is the foundation of everything here. Exotic pet ownership carries responsibility, and that means making smart,compassionate choices—not just for your pet, but for the environment too. We'll talk about how to be a thoughtful, responsible owner who contributes to conservation, not harm.

So,are you ready to dive in? With me by your side, you'll discover the joys and challenges of life with an exotic pet. You'll build a unique bond with a creature unlike any other—and your life just might get a little more magical because of it. Let's begin this wild journey together. After all, who doesn't want a little more adventure in their every day?

Chapter 1: Choosing Your Exotic Companion

Matching Personality and Lifestyle with the Perfect Pet

You know that moment when you walk into a pet store and suddenly a bright green iguana gives you the side-eye, as if to say, "I dare you to take me home"? It's like they're casting a spell, luring you into their world of scales, feathers, and the occasional tail whip. Choosing an exotic pet is a bit like picking your Hogwarts house. You want to ensure the choice aligns with your lifestyle and personality, because your new friend might just be sticking around for a while, and you don't want to end up with a Slytherin when you're more of a Hufflepuff kind of person. But take a step back before you let that iguana work its magic on you. Choosing an exotic pet isn't just about impulse; it's about understanding what you truly want from this experience.

Understanding Your Motivation for Exotic Pet Ownership

Before you leap into the enchanting realm of exotic pets, take a moment to ask yourself, "Why do I want an exotic pet?" It's not just a matter of vanity or wanting something more extraordinary than your neighbor's goldfish. Exotic pets offer a unique companionship that, while fulfilling, comes with its own set of challenges. Perhaps you're seeking the emotional bond a parrot can offer, with its chatty demeanor and ability to pick up the latest pop song. Or maybe you're drawn to the novelty and distinction of owning a creature that most people only see in nature documentaries or their wildest dreams.

Owning an exotic pet is a long-term commitment, akin to signing up for a gym membership that you can't simply cancel when the year ends. These pets can live for decades, meaning you're in for the long haul. Be prepared for some lifestyle adjustments—such as rearranging your living room to accommodate a terrarium or learning to appreciate the sound of crickets (the ones you feed your gecko, that is). Exotic pets require specific care, including a tailored diet, suitable habitat, and regular veterinary attention, which isn't a onetime setup but an ongoing responsibility.

Think of yourself as a conservationist at home. Every choice you make—from where your pet comes from to how you care for it—affects not just one animal, but entire ecosystems. You must keep everything running smoothly without compromising your pet's welfare. These animals often originate from delicate ecosystems, and taking one home means considering the impact on its natural habitat. Supporting ethical breeding practices is essential, as it ensures the well-being of the animals and supports conservation efforts. Irresponsible breeding can lead to health issues and reduce genetic diversity, which is a big no-no if you want your pet to thrive.

So, how do you know if you're truly ready to bring home a rare and wonderful creature? Begin with a self-assessment. Evaluate the time and energy you're willing to dedicate. Exotic pets aren't just weekend projects; they need your attention daily. Consider your financial readiness, too. Between food, specialized enclosures, heating, and vet care, some exotic pets can cost hundreds—sometimes thousands—annually. That bearded dragon might be cheaper than a puppy upfront, but over its 10–to 15-year lifespan. Not so much. Create a checklist to ensure you're prepared for the commitment, both emotionally and practically.

Take a moment to reflect on your motivations and readiness. Are you looking for a friend who will never judge your Netflix choices or someone to share your quiet moments with? Understanding your reasons will guide you to the right companion. Consider this your exotic pet pre-flight checklist: If you've nodded along, congratulations—you're already thinking like a responsible owner of exotic pets. Let's find the perfect companion for your wild and wonderful adventure. Welcome to the adventurous, sometimes unpredictable, but always rewarding world of exotic pet ownership.

Navigating the Exotic Pet Marketplace: Ethical Choices

The exotic pet marketplace is a dazzling labyrinth where the lure of rare creatures can sometimes cloud judgment. Sellers flash tempting offers,

5 Safety Tips

rare finds, and limited-time deals, but the genuine treasure lies in making choices, prioritizing animal welfare over impulse.. It's a world where sellers may try to dazzle you with the allure of rare species, making it all too easy to lose sight of what's most important: the welfare of the animals and the integrity of your choices. The key to navigating this wilderness is focusing on ethical breeders and sellers, prioritizing transparency and animal welfare over flashy sales tactics. So, how do you spot these ethical supports among the crowd? Start by scrutinizing pet advertisements. If a seller promises a "super rare" creature at a bargain price, consider it a red flag waving furiously. Ethical breeders won't pressure you with scarcity tactics or rush you into making a purchase. Instead, they provide honest information about the animal's origin, health, and care requirements.

Next, do some detective work on breeder reputations. In today's digital age, reviews and testimonials are your most valuable assets. A quick online search can reveal a great deal about a seller's track record. Look for consistent positive feedback, particularly regarding the health and temperament of their animals. Ask the breeder questions. Reputable sellers encourage inquiries and are transparent about their breeding practices. They understand that an informed buyer is a responsible owner, so they are happy to share details about their animals' living conditions, diet, and veterinary care. Ethical breeders often collaborate closely with conservation organizations, focusing on preserving genetic diversity and promoting the health of their species. They aim to produce well-adjusted pets that thrive in captive environments rather than just turning a profit.

Why Ethical Sourcing Matters:

- The illegal exotic pet trade fuels habitat destruction and endangers wild populations.

- Ethical breeders prioritize conservation, responsible breeding, and minimizing the risks of inbreeding.

- Supporting regulated, responsible sources protect animals and the environment.

Ethical breeders often have transparent sales practices and avoid selling to unsuitable owners, ensuring a positive impact on the pet and its natural environment. Supporting these breeders promotes animal welfare and helps conserve endangered species. This approach helps reduce the risk of inbreeding-related health issues, supporting the long-term viability of captive populations.

When assessing potential pet sellers, use a checklist to evaluate their credibility and ethics. Ensure they provide transparent information about the animal's origin and health history. Confirm that they offer ongoing support and education for new owners, helping you understand the challenges and requirements of caring for exotic pets. They must adhere to ethical breeding practices, focusing on animal welfare over profit. Legal compliance is another critical aspect of ethical pet ownership. Before purchasing an exotic pet, familiarize yourself

With local and international laws. This knowledge is not just a formality; it's a necessity. Different species often have unique legal restrictions, and owning certain animals without the proper permits can lead to severe consequences. These might include fines, confiscation of the pet, or even legal action. Understanding and adhering to these laws ensures the safety and well-being of both your pet and the broader community.

You might need a license to own specific exotic pets in some regions, while others may have outright bans. Ensure you are aware of the local requirements before bringing an exotic animal home. Choosing legal and ethical sources contributes to a more sustainable and responsible pet trade. This benefits the animals themselves, supports broader conservation efforts, and maintains the delicate balance of natural ecosystems. Your choices as a pet owner matter—not just to your future pet, but to the ecosystem it came from. Before making a purchase, take a moment to research, ask questions, and ensure you're making an ethical decision. The health of our planet and the well-being of exotic animals depend on informed, responsible owners like you.

Lifestyle Compatibility: Matching Pets to Your Routine

Imagine being amid a bustling day, barely having time to sip your morning coffee, and suddenly remembering your new pet iguana needs its daily dose of UVB light and a fresh salad. Balancing the care of exotic pets with daily life is an art. It all starts with understanding how your lifestyle aligns with your pet's needs.

First, consider space. A ball python is happy in a modest terrarium, but a green iguana is not.? You might need a setup that rivals your living room decor. Consider the dynamics if you've got a bustling household with kids and other pets. A friendly bearded dragon might make the perfect interactive family member, while a more solitary creature, such as a leopard gecko, may prefer to retreat from the commotion.

Owning an exotic pet isn't just about finding space for a cage or tank. It's also about the time and resources you're willing to invest. High-maintenance species require daily attention, from feeding to habitat maintenance, whereas low-maintenance pets may only need weekly check-ins. Financially speaking, think of exotic pets as the luxury cars of the animal world.

Estimated Costs of Exotic Pet Ownership:

- Enclosure Setup: $200–$1,000+ (Custom-built habitats for larger reptiles can be costly!)

- Food: $20–$100/month (Live insects, specialty diets)

- Heating & Lighting: $50–$300 upfront, plus electricity costs

- Specialized exotic vets charge $100–$300 per checkup

- Ongoing Maintenance: $20–$100/month (Cleaning supplies, substrate replacement)

Creating a budget for these expenses ensures you're prepared for everything from routine check-ups to unexpected emergencies, much like setting aside a rainy-day fund.

Integrating a pet into your life may seem daunting for those juggling hectic schedules, but fear not! There are strategies to make it work. Designing a pet-friendly living space doesn't mean sacrificing style for function. With some creativity, you can create a habitat that blends seamlessly with your home, turning your chameleon's enclosure into a centerpiece rather than an eyesore. For busy bees, flexibility is key. Implementing a care schedule that accommodates work and family commitments can help prevent pet care from becoming a chore. Perhaps mornings are for feeding and evenings for quality interaction time, allowing you to unwind in the company of your scaly or feathered friend.

Now, let's discuss matchmaking in the pet world. If you're a busy professional with little time to spare, consider low-maintenance reptiles like corn snakes or leopard geckos. They don't demand constant attention and are content with a simple routine. If you thrive on social interaction and have a lively household, an interactive bird like a cockatiel might be your perfect match. These birds take pleasure in interacting with their human companions and bring a cheerful presence to any room. For those who crave companionship without the fuss, axolotls provide a charming, low-maintenance option, thriving in a simple aquatic setup with minimal care requirements.

Lifestyle-Pet Compatibility Quiz

Find your perfect exotic pet match by answering the following questions:

1. How much space can you dedicate to your pet's habitat?

    a. A corner of a room.

    b. An entire room, a small section of my yard.

2. How much time can you spend daily on pet care?

    a. Less than 30 minutes

    b. 30 minutes to 1 hour

    c. Over 1 hour

3. Are there children or other pets in your home?

    a. No, it's just me

    b. . Yes, children

    c. Yes, other pets

4. What is your budget for the initial setup and ongoing care?

    a. Minimal: I'm on a tight budget.

    b. Moderate: I'm willing to spend a bit.

    c. Generous: money isn't a significant concern.

Use your answers to guide your pet selection process, ensuring your new exotic friend fits seamlessly into your life.

The Importance of Species-Specific Research

Now that you've considered your lifestyle, let's discuss the next crucial step: research.

Imagine bringing home an exotic pet without knowing much about it—like trying to bake a souffle without a recipe. You might end up with a confused iguana, wondering why its terrarium feels more like a sauna!

Proper research ensures you're prepared for your pet's daily care and long-term well-being.

Each species has unique quirks and needs, and understanding these can make all the difference between a thriving pet and one that merely survives. Dive into reputable sources for your species of choice—books, websites, and perhaps even a chat with the knowledgeable staff member at your local pet store who seems to know everything. Consult exotic pet experts; they've seen it all and can provide insights you won't find in your average pet care book. You wouldn't trust anyone to do your taxes, so why trust just anyone with your pet's well-being?

Now, let's delve into the specifics of species-specific care. Think of it like tailoring a suit—one size doesn't fit at all. Reptiles, for instance, often require precise temperature and humidity levels to mimic their natural habitats. A bearded dragon might bask contentedly under a warm lamp, but a chameleon needs a misty environment to feel right at home. Dietary needs also vary significantly. Some reptiles are insectivores, meaning they feast on a diet rich in crickets and mealworms, while others might relish a salad of fresh greens. Social needs differ, too. While some birds thrive in bustling environments with plenty of interaction, other species, like certain snakes, prefer a more solitary existence. Understanding these nuances ensures you provide an environment that feels like a home, not just a cage.

But what happens if you skip the research? Imagine setting up a habitat for a snake without realizing it needs a secure lid, only to find it exploring your living room in the middle of the night. Improper care can lead to health risks, ranging from respiratory infections resulting from incorrect humidity levels to nutritional deficiencies caused by an inadequate diet. Behavioral issues can arise as well. A parrot that isn't mentally stimulated might resort to feather plucking, while a stressed gecko might refuse to eat. You can avoid these challenges with homework, saving yourself unnecessary stress and vet bills.

To continue learning, take advantage of the wealth of resources available to you. Join online forums where exotic pet enthusiasts gather to swap stories and advice. Subscribe to scientific journals on herpetology, which can provide insights into the latest research and care techniques. Books are invaluable, too. A well-written guide can serve as a trusted advisor and a bedtime read. Online and in-person communities offer support and camaraderie, turning a solitary interest into a shared passion. It's like having a book club, but instead of discussing the latest bestseller, you're swapping tips on the best substrate for your ball python enclosure.

In this vibrant world of exotic pet ownership, becoming informed is an ongoing adventure. Your pet relies on you to understand its world, and with the right tools and knowledge, you can ensure it leads a whole, happy life. Keep your curiosity alive; remember, there's always more to learn.

What's your next step?

- Research your top pet choices.

- Begin by visiting a reputable breeder or rescue organization.

- Setting up a habitat that meets your future pet's needs.

- Your journey into exotic pet ownership starts now. "Are you ready?"

- Exploring the Personality Traits of Popular Exotic Pets.

Picture this: you're on your couch, sipping your morning coffee, when your parrot, perched nearby, decides it's time to chat. It mimics your laugh, asks if you want a cracker, and then criticizes your choice of breakfast cereal. Parrots are like stand-up comedians of the pet world—always seeking interaction and attention. Their social tendencies mean they thrive on engagement, often requiring daily conversations and activities to maintain their happiness. They're the life of the party, but owning one means you've signed up for a lifetime of witty banter and the occasional unsolicited opinion on your wardrobe choices.

However, not all exotic pets require being the center of attention. Certain reptiles are a perfect fit if you prefer a low-maintenance, independent companion. Take the ball python, for instance. These introverted creatures are content with their own company, basking in their enclosures and occasionally emerging to explore leisurely. They're the ten masters of the reptile world, preferring calm and solitude. Similarly, crested geckos are nocturnal and independent. They'll happily observe you from their enclosure but rarely seek interaction. Instead of demanding your attention, they prefer the quiet life—climbing branches under the cover of darkness and occasionally giving you a curious side-eye.

Your exotic pet's personality traits can profoundly shape your relationship. Intelligent species, such as parrots and certain reptiles, require interactive engagement and mental stimulation to thrive. This means you'll need to invest time in teaching tricks or providing puzzles to keep their minds engaged and their brains busy. Ignoring their need for interaction can lead to boredom or behavioral issues, like leaving a toddler alone with a permanent marker and a blank wall. Introverted pets, such as certain snakes or geckos, appreciate a quieter existence. They demand respect for their personal space and thrive when their routines remain undisturbed.

Understanding Exotic Pet Body Language

Interpreting pet behaviors, including head bobs, tail flicks, and subtle changes in posture, is like learning a new language. Recognizing these cues can help you understand your pet's mood and needs more effectively.

1. Common Exotic Pet Body Language:

2. Parrots: Flaring feathers = excitement OR aggression.

3. Bearded Dragons: Head bobs = dominance; Arm waving = submission.

4. Snakes: Tightly coiled body = stress; Flicking tongue = curiosity.

Positive reinforcement training can also be an effective tool for shaping desirable behaviors. Use treats and praise to reward actions you want to encourage; however, remember patience is key—Rome wasn't built in a day, and neither is a well-mannered parrot.

Consider the story of a friend's sulcata tortoise, who developed a fondness for following her around the garden. Initially shy, this tortoise grew more confident with gentle encouragement and a few leafy greens as bribes. Over time, it became a charming companion, showcasing a curious and endearing personality. Then there's the tale of a leopard gecko named Spot, who refused to eat for days after a move. A simple change in habitat setup—adding a few more hiding spots—transformed Spot from a grumpy recluse into a happy, well-adjusted gecko.

These anecdotes highlight how understanding and adapting to your pet's personality can foster a strong bond. Some owners even find that their pets' quirks and habits mirror their own, creating a unique connection built on mutual understanding.

Exotic pets may not wag their tails or purr, but they have their ways of communicating affection and contentment—if you know how to listen.

What's Next?

Next time you interact with your pet, pay close attention. Are they watching you curiously? Responding to your voice? Flicking their tail with excitement? Understanding their personality and behavior deepens your bond and makes pet ownership even more rewarding!

Personalized Pet Selection Tool: Finding Your Perfect Match

Imagine standing in front of a wall of terrariums, each housing a more fascinating creature than the last. You feel like a kid in a candy store, but instead of sugary confections, you face the dilemma of choosing between a bearded dragon and a corn snake. How do you decide which companion suits you best?

Enter our Personalized Pet Selection Tool—a helpful guide to assist you in making this exciting decision with confidence. This tool functions like a matchmaking service, but for pets. By answering a series of questions about your lifestyle, preferences, and home environment, you can pinpoint the perfect exotic pet for you. It's all about compatibility, ensuring you and your new friend are a match made in reptilian heaven.

How This Works

Before exploring specific pet recommendations, take a moment to reflect on your daily habits and lifestyle. Do you want a pet that actively seeks interaction or one that's content with minimal handling? Would you prefer a pet that's awake when you are, or does a nocturnal schedule fit better with your routine?

We use an algorithm-based compatibility scoring system that weighs factors, such as your daily routine, available living space, and desired pet characteristics. Perhaps you're an introvert who prefers the calm presence of a tortoise, or maybe you're an energetic extrovert looking for an active bird to keep you company. Our tool takes these aspects into account, matching you with a pet that fits seamlessly into your life.

Find Your Perfect Exotic Pet

Answer the following questions to discover your ideal match!

1. How much time can you dedicate to your pet daily?

1. Less than 30 minutes

2. 30–60 minutes

3. Over an hour

2. How do you feel about handling your pet?
   1. I prefer a hands-off pet

   2. Occasionally, but not too much

   3. I love interactive pets!

3. When are you most active?
   1. Mornings

   2. Afternoons

   3. Evenings / Night

4. How much space do you have?
   1. Small apartment

   2. A room for an enclosure

   3. Plenty of space

Results:

Mostly As'? A low-maintenance, independent pet, such as a ball python, crested gecko, or tarantula, is a great fit.

Mostly Bs'? You might enjoy a semi-interactive pet, such as a bearded dragon, tortoise, or leopard gecko.

Mostly Cs'? A social pet like a parrot, ferret, or iguana would suit your lifestyle!

Chapter 2:
Habitat Setup and Maintenance

Creating Safe, Comfortable, and Stimulating Spaces

I magine your exotic pet's enclosure as a tiny slice of paradise in your living room. It's a bit like designing a dream home for a critter who doesn't care about wallpaper or plumbing. Welcome to the world of bioactive setups, where each tank transforms into a self-sustaining ecosystem, practically a mini-rainforest or desert, depending on your pet's preferences. These setups are not just a fad; they are a revolution in pet care. They mimic the natural environment, reducing maintenance to the occasional pat on the back—or the occasional cleaning of terrarium glass.

Bioactive enclosures are the ultimate multitaskers. They break down waste naturally, thanks to a hardworking crew of tiny critters known as microfauna. Think of them as your pet's cleaning staff. Springtails and isopods might not wear little maid outfits, but they - efficiently decompose waste, keeping the habitat clean and fresh. This natural waste breakdown reduces odors and the need for frequent cleaning, allowing you to spend more time enjoying your pet's antics and less time scrubbing walls. Plus, the complexity of these setups stimulates your pet's mind, offering enrichment through a dynamic environment filled with live plants and natural textures.

Setting up a bioactive habitat is like baking a cake—there's a recipe, and each layer matters. First, choose the right enclosure size. It should be spacious enough to let your pet roam, but cozy enough to maintain a stable environment. Next, pick a substrate that supports both plant growth and microfauna. Coconut fiber, plantation soil, or a mix of moss and sand can create a fertile ground for plants while welcoming the microfauna that will call it home. Using materials like bio-drain substrate, you'll also need a drainage layer to prevent water-logging and keep the roots happy. Once you've laid the groundwork, it's time to add live plants. These aren't just for decoration; they play a crucial role in the ecosystem by absorbing carbon dioxide and releasing oxygen, much like a tiny botanical garden.

Microfauna, the unsung heroes of your bioactive setup, plays a crucial role in maintaining balance. These are your detritivores, such as springtails and isopods, which may sound like the names of alien species, but they are integral to your ecosystem. Springtails are tiny, wingless insects that thrive in moist environments, breaking down, decomposing organic matter. Isopods, often referred to as "pill bugs" or "sow bugs," feed on decaying plant material, thereby aiding in waste management. Cultivating these populations is simple. Introduce them to your substrate and maintain consistent humidity levels. They'll multiply and maintain the tank's cleanliness, allowing your pet to live in a pristine environment without you having to lift a finger.

Maintaining a bioactive setup requires a bit of observation and occasional tweaks. Monitor plant health by checking for growth and any signs of wilting. A thriving plant is usually a good indicator of a healthy ecosystem. Adjust humidity levels to support plant life and microfauna, ensuring the environment remains stable. It's not unusual to feel like a gardener and a zookeeper all in one, perhaps without the big hat. Monitor your microfauna populations as well. If they appear to be dwindling, it may show an imbalance in the ecosystem that needs to be addressed.

Bioactive Setup Checklist

A bioactive setup transforms your pet's enclosure into a self-sustaining ecosystem—practically a mini-rainforest or desert, depending on their natural habitat. This method reduces maintenance, improves air quality, and provides enrichment.

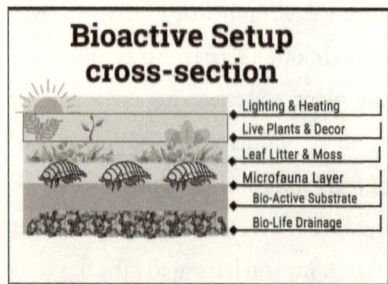

Why Choose a Bioactive Enclosure?

1. Natural Waste Breakdown: Springtails & isopods act as your pet's "cleaning staff," decomposing waste and keeping the habitat fresh.

2. Odor Control: Reduces smell by naturally breaking down organic matter.

3. Less Maintenance: No more frequent deep cleaning—just occasional upkeep.

4. Enrichment for Your Pet: Live plants and textures mimic the wild, stimulating your pet's mind.

5. Setting Up a Bioactive Habitat: Step-by-Step.

. Choose the Right Enclosure Size

- Must be spacious enough for movement, hiding, and basking.

- Small enclosures can stress active species like bearded dragons.

. Select the Proper Substrate

- Must support plant growth and microfauna.

- Best options: Coconut fiber, plantation soil, or a mix of moss and sand.

. Add a Drainage Layer

- Prevent water-logging and root rot.

- Use: Clay balls, bio-drain substrate, or a false bottom system.

. Introduce Live Plants

- Choose safe plants based on humidity & temperature needs.

- Examples: Pothos, ferns, and bromeliads for high humidity; succulents for dry environments.

. Introduce Microfauna (Clean-Up Crew)

- Springtails: Tiny decomposers that thrive in moisture.

- Isopods ("pill bugs") Break down plant material & aerate the soil.

- These reduce waste buildup and prevent mold growth.

. Monitor & Maintain Stability

- Watch plant health for signs of imbalance.

- Ensure humidity levels remain stable.

- Observe microfauna populations—if declining, replenish as needed.

Bioactive Setup Checklist

- Enclosure Size: Is it spacious enough for movement and comfort?

- Substrate Layer: Supports the growth of plants and microfauna?

- Drainage System: Prevents water logging?

- Live Plants: Safe and thriving?

- Microfauna: Springtails and isopods introduced.

- Humidity Levels: Are they stable and within the ideal range?

With these basics, your bioactive setup will flourish, providing your pet with a natural and enriching home.

Temperature and Humidity Control: Creating a Balanced Environment

Temperature and humidity aren't just buzzwords thrown around by weather forecasters, they're the lifeblood of your exotic pet habitat. Imagine your pet as a tiny diva, demanding the perfect climate to thrive, like Goldilocks in a terrarium. Too hot, too cold, too dry, or too humid, and you might find yourself with a grumpy gecko or a sulking snake. Fluctuating temperatures can disrupt your pet's metabolism. It is like trying to run a marathon while juggling ice packs and hot water bottles. Your pet requires a consistent climate to regulate its body processes, ensuring it can digest food properly and maintain optimal energy levels. Humidity plays a crucial role, especially in supporting respiratory health. If there is too little moisture, your pet might struggle, as if it's walking through a desert; too much, and it could feel submerged in a tropical swamp.

To maintain this delicate balance, you'll need a few gadgets that seem to belong in a sci-fi movie. Meet your new best friends: the digital thermometer and hygrometer. These nifty devices keep tabs on temperature and humidity, ensuring you're always in the know. A thermostat can be your secret weapon, allowing you to set and maintain the ideal temperature without constantly fiddling with heat lamps or pads. Humidifiers can help rescue you when the air becomes too dry, adding moisture to aid your pet's breathing. It's all about creating a harmonious environment where your pet feels at home, not stuck in a sauna or an igloo.

Now, let's talk specifically. Different species have different needs, so tailoring the habitat to your unique critter is crucial. Reptiles, for instance, often prefer a basking area where temperatures soar above 100°F, allowing them to soak up the warmth like sunbathers on the beach. Amphibians might crave a cooler, more humid environment, relishing in the atmosphere that would make a human reach for a raincoat. Like the ever-popular crested gecko, tropical species thrive in high humidity, enjoying levels between 70% and 80%. Meanwhile, desert dwellers like the bearded dragon are content with a drier setting, around 30% to 40% humidity, much like a well-air-conditioned room in the summer.

Even with the best intentions, you might encounter a hiccup or two. Recognizing heat stress or humidity issues early can make all the difference. A pet that's too hot may display lethargy or open-mouth breathing, while one that's too cold could become sluggish or refuse to eat. If humidity levels drop too low, your pet might struggle with shedding, like wearing a sweater two sizes too small. Too much humidity can lead to mold and respiratory infections. To combat these problems, adjust ventilation by opening or closing vents or repositioning the enclosure away from direct sunlight or drafts. Sometimes, minor tweaks can restore balance, ensuring your pet remains comfortable and healthy.

Creating the perfect habitat is fine-tuning and paying attention to your pet's cues. Like a well-oiled machine, a balanced environment will keep your pet thriving, allowing it to bask in paradise. With the right tools and knowledge, you can transform your pet's habitat into a sanctuary where it can flourish, free from the stresses of an inhospitable climate.

Temperature and humidity aren't just buzzwords thrown around by weather forecasters; they're the lifeblood of your pet's habitat.

Imagine your pet as a tiny diva, demanding the perfect climate to thrive, like Goldilocks in a terrarium. Too hot, too cold, too dry, or too humid? You might find yourself with a grumpy gecko or a sulking snake.

Why It Matters:

✔ Regulates digestion & metabolism

✔ Prevents respiratory issues & skin shedding problems

✔ Mimics natural seasonal changes for breeding & health

Essential Tools for Temperature & Humidity Management

- Digital Thermometer & Hygrometer–Track temp & humidity accurately.

- Thermostat–Controls heat sources to prevent overheating.

30

- Humidifier/Mister–Adds moisture for tropical species.

- Ventilation Adjustments–Increase airflow to reduce excess humidity.

- Species-Specific Temperature & Humidity Guide.

Signs of Temperature or Humidity Issues:
- Too Hot? Lethargy, open-mouth breathing, excessive hiding.

- Too Cold? Sluggishness, refusal to eat, excessive burrowing.

- Too Dry? Poor shedding, dull skin.

- Too Humid? Mold growth, respiratory issues.

Lighting Essentials: The Role of UVB and Heat Lamps

Imagine your exotic pet's enclosure as a cozy little stage with lighting as crucial as the set design. Proper lighting is not just about making your pet look good; it's essential for their overall health. Let's start with UVB lighting. It's the backstage hero, pivotal in calcium metabolism, ensuring your pet's bones are as sturdy as a rock. Without it, your reptile might develop a metabolic bone disease, which is as unpleasant as it sounds. UVB rays help your pet synthesize vitamin D3, crucial for calcium absorption. It's like giving them a daily dose of sunshine without the risk of sunburn. Then we have heat lamps, basically your pet's sun. These lamps provide the warmth necessary for thermoregulation, allowing your cold-blooded friend to control its body temperature. Imagine trying to warm up after a chilly swim without the luxury of a cozy blanket—heat lamps offer that essential warmth.

Selecting the right lighting products can feel like choosing the perfect pair of sunglasses, which is fashionable yet functional. You've got options like fluorescent and mercury vapor bulbs. Fluorescent bulbs, compact or tube-style, are great for smaller enclosures or specific areas. They're easy to install and offer a sharp lighting gradient. Mercury vapor bulbs provide both UVB and heat, making them the Swiss Army knife of reptile lighting. They're ideal for larger enclosures where you want to mimic the blazing desert sun. When selecting a brand, opt for reputable names that promise longevity and reliability. Some species, such as bearded dragons or tortoises, may prefer T5 UVB lights because of their brighter output and extended range. This setup ensures that even the most sun-loving creatures receive their daily dose of sunlight.

Now, where should you place all these lights? Think of it as arranging furniture in your living room strategically and thoughtfully. The distance between the light source and your pet is crucial. Too close, and your pet might feel like it's in a sauna; too far, and it might not get the full benefits. Aim for a sweet spot where the UVB and heat reach their intended targets without overwhelming your pet. You can use timers to create natural day-night cycles, ensuring your pet doesn't feel like it's living in Alaska during the summer months with endless daylight. These cycles help regulate their sleep and activity patterns, making them feel right at home.

But be warned—Excessive or insufficient light causes problems. Without adequate UVB, your pet risks developing metabolic bone disease, which can lead to bone deformities and weakness. It's like trying to build a house with brittle bricks. Conversely, excessive heat can lead to stress and dehydration, leaving your pet feeling as though they are stuck in the Sahara. Continuously monitor the enclosure's temperature and adjust as needed. If your pet acts sluggish or avoiding its basking area, these might be signs of overheating or discomfort. It's all about finding that Goldilocks zone where everything is just right.

Ultimately, lighting your pet's habitat is an art and a science. With the right choices, you can create a visually appealing environment that perfectly suits your pet's needs.

Placing lights correctly is like arranging furniture in your living room—it must be strategic and functional.

Positioning UVB Lights

- Too Close? Your pet is at risk of overexposure, which can lead to eye damage.

- Too Far? The UVB rays become ineffective, leading to vitamin deficiencies.

- *The Sweet Spot? Typically 10–12 inches from the basking area, but refer to the manufacturer's guidelines for exact measurements.*

Heat Lamp Setup

- Create a temperature gradient—a warmer basking area (90–110°F) and a cooler retreat zone.

- Use a thermostat to regulate the heat and avoid overheating.

Set a Natural Day-Night Cycle

Using timers to replicate a natural sunrise and sunset helps your pet maintain a healthy sleep-wake cycle. Without it, they might feel as though they're living in Alaska's endless summer, feeling confused and restless.

Avoiding Common Lighting Mistakes

- Not Enough UVB?

- Warning Signs: weak bones, sluggish movement, deformed limbs.

- Fix: Upgrade to a more pungent UVB bulb and ensure unobstructed exposure (no glass barriers).

Overheating the Enclosure?

- Warning Signs: Avoiding basking spots, excessive hiding, and dehydration.

- Fix: Use a thermostat, adjust bulb placement, and provide shaded areas.

Too Much or Too Little Light?

- Warning Signs: Unusual sleep patterns, loss of appetite, and stress.

- Fix: Maintain 12-hour light cycles, ensuring gradual dimming at night.

Substrates and Decor: Crafting a Natural Habitat

Designing the perfect habitat for your exotic pet is like crafting a miniature version of the great outdoors. Substrates and decor are not just fancy words for dirt and doodads; they're the backbone of a comfortable and enriching environment. Let's start with substrates. Think of them as the carpet for your pet's little mansion, providing comfort and a medium for natural behaviors. Whether it's a bearded dragon joyfully kicking up sand or a gecko burrowing into coconut fiber, the right substrate encourages these instinctual activities. It's not just about aesthetics; substrates also serve as a visual barrier, reducing stress by allowing your pet to hide away from the world when it needs a little "me time."

Selecting the right substrate is crucial, much like choosing between shag carpet or hardwood floors for your own home. For tropical species, coconut fiber is a fantastic choice. It keeps moisture, helping maintain that lush, humid environment reminiscent of a rain-soaked jungle. For desert-dwelling reptiles, sand substrates are ideal, replicating their arid homeland where they can dig and explore. Whatever you choose, ensure it's safe and non-toxic. Avoid substrates with tiny particles that can cause impaction if ingested—your pet's tummy will thank you. Constantly tailor substrate choices to the specific needs of your pet species, considering their natural habitat and behaviors.

Think of substrates as the foundation of your pet's home, like choosing between carpet or hardwood floors for your house. They provide:

- Comfort & Support—A cushioned surface for movement & burrowing.

- Environmental Regulation—Helps keep moisture or replicate dry terrain.

- Enrichment—Encourages natural behaviors like digging & hiding.

- Quick Substrate Guide: Best Picks for Different Pets.

Avoid These: Small particle substrates, such as crushed walnut shells and fine sand, can cause impaction (digestive blockages). Always research species-specific needs before selecting a substrate!

Now, onto decor.

Decor isn't just for Instagram-worthy enclosures—it provides security, exercise, and mental stimulation.

- Hides & Shelters: All animals need a safe retreat to reduce stress.

- Climbing Structures: For arboreal species (like chameleons), branches & vines encourage natural movement.

- Natural vs. Artificial Plants: Live plants help regulate humidity, while artificial ones provide low-maintenance cover.

- Pro Tip: Securely place all decor to prevent tipping hazards. A falling hide or unstable branch can injure your pet!

These features make the habitat visually appealing and enhance your pet's overall experience. Just picture your snake elegantly draped over a branch or your chameleon blending into a leafy backdrop—it's like a scene from a nature documentary right in your living room,

Keeping your substrates and decor clean is akin to maintaining your living room. Regular substrate replacement is vital to prevent odor buildup and maintain hygiene. Depending on the species and setup, you might need to change the substrate weekly or bi-weekly, especially if your pet enjoys redecorating with its dinner leftovers. When decorating, a simple rinse with warm water often does the trick, but a diluted vinegar solution can work wonders for stubborn grime. Be wary of harsh chemicals that could harm your pet. These should be part of your regular cleaning routine if you have artificial plants or hiding spots. Ensure they're securely placed to prevent unfortunate toppling incidents, which could turn a cozy hideaway into an accidental obstacle course.

Maintaining a natural habitat might seem like a lot of work, but the rewards are worth it. Watching your pet thrive in an environment that closely mimics its natural one is incredibly satisfying. It's all about creating a space that meets your pet's physical and psychological needs. Whether it's a sandy nook for a tortoise or a leafy canopy for a tree frog, the proper setup can transform your pet's enclosure into a sanctuary that supports its well-being and enriches its life.

Maintenance Routines: Keeping Habitats Clean and Safe

Think of your pet's enclosure as a bustling little city—your pet is the mayor, and you're the city planner & sanitation crew. Regular cleaning helps prevent the buildup of harmful bacteria and keeps your pet's environment safe.

Keeping the habitat clean isn't just about aesthetics; it's crucial for your pet's health and safety. Dirty environments can lead to the buildup of harmful pathogens, which are like invisible villains waiting to wreak havoc on your pet's immune system. By managing waste and odors effectively, you create a sanctuary where your pet can thrive without the risk of illness lurking around the corner.

Creating a structured maintenance schedule is like drafting a foolproof plan for success. Daily tasks might include checking the water and food for cleanliness, because nobody wants to drink day-old water, not even your pet lizard. It's also essential to remove any uneaten food to prevent it from becoming a breeding ground for bacteria. Weekly, perform substrate spot cleaning. This involves removing any soiled areas, which is akin to changing the sheets on your pet's bed. Depending on the type of substrate, you may also need to fluff it up slightly to keep it fresh and inviting. Monthly, it's time for a deeper clean, which can include washing the entire enclosure and replacing large sections of substrate. Think of it as spring cleaning, only your pet doesn't get to stuff everything under the bed when company comes over .

For cleaning, safety first should be your mantra. Using non-toxic cleaning solutions is key to ensuring that you're not inadvertently introducing harmful chemicals. A humble mixture of vinegar and water works wonders for disinfecting surfaces without posing a threat to your pet. This natural solution is effective against germs and odors, and it's gentle enough to use regularly. When using commercial cleaning products, choose those specifically for pet environments and follow instructions carefully. Safe handling of these chemicals includes wearing gloves, ensuring proper ventilation, and thoroughly rinsing all surfaces before allowing your pet back into its pristine palace.

Simpler maintenance doesn't mean doing less work. Implementing bioactive elements can significantly streamline routine care tasks. These natural systems help break down waste, reducing the frequency of deep cleans. For water-based habitats, consider using automated systems for water changes. These devices can help maintain water quality by automatically removing and replacing a portion of the water, much like an invisible butler who ensures everything is just so. Not only does this save time, but it also maintains the stability of the environment, which is crucial for sensitive aquatic species. Simple organizational tools, such as keeping a checklist or setting reminders, can help keep you on track and prevent maintenance lapses.

Ultimately, maintaining a clean and safe habitat is about creating a balanced routine that fits seamlessly into your lifestyle. With the right approach, you can ensure that your pet's home remains a sanctuary where it can thrive in comfort and health, free from neglect or disorder.

Structured Cleaning Routine: Daily, Weekly, & Monthly Tasks

Daily Cleaning Checklist:

1. Remove uneaten food—Prevents mold & bacteria buildup.

2. Check water quality—Replace dirty water with fresh, clean water.

3. Spot clean waste—Scoop up soiled substrate or droppings.

Weekly Maintenance:

1. Substrate spot-cleaning—Remove dirty areas, such as when changing pet bedding.

2. Wipe down surfaces—Use a diluted vinegar solution or reptile-safe cleaner.

3. Inspect plants & decor—Look for mold, damage, or signs of pests.

Monthly Deep Clean:

- Replace large sections of substrate—Prevents bacteria buildup.

- Wash & disinfect decor—Scrub hides, climbing structures, and artificial plants.

- Check humidity and ventilation—Ensure the environment remains stable and mold-free.

Cleaning Safety: What to Use & What to Avoid

Using the right cleaning products is just as important as cleaning itself.

Safe Cleaning Solutions:

1. Diluted White Vinegar & Water—A natural disinfectant, safe for most enclosures.

2. Pet-Safe Enclosure Cleaners—Specifically designed to kill bacteria without harming pets.

3. Hot Water & Scrubbing—Works well for routine maintenance.

Avoid These!

- Bleach & Ammonia—Can cause respiratory issues if not thoroughly rinsed.

- Scented Cleaners—Many contain toxic chemicals that are

harmful to reptiles and amphibians.

- Abrasive Scrubbers—Can scratch glass & plastic surfaces, trapping bacteria.

Reducing Maintenance Workload: Work Smarter, Not Harder

Want to clean less while keeping the enclosure pristine? Here's how:

✔ Go Bioactive! — Introduce clean-up crews, such as springtails and isopods, to break down waste naturally.

✔ Use Automated Water Systems—Great for aquatic species, as they maintain water quality effortlessly.

✔ Keep a Checklist—Set reminders for weekly & monthly deep cleans.

Troubleshooting Habitat Challenges: Common Issues and Solutions

Even the best-laid plans can go awry, especially when it comes to the cozy little ecosystems we create for our exotic friends. One moment, you're admiring your gecko as it lounges on its favorite branch, and the next, you're met with a suspicious patch of mold creeping up the enclosure wall. Mold loves humid environments, which your tropical pets likely require, but your goal is to maintain a balance that supports your pet's health without inviting unwanted guests. Mold thrives when moisture levels are high and airflow is poor, turning your pet's home into a fungi paradise. Meanwhile, bioactive setups may face pest infestations as uninvited bugs decide to crash your perfectly curated

ecosystem, feasting on organic material and sometimes bothering your pe
t.

To tackle these challenges, start by focusing on airflow. Improving ventilation can significantly reduce mold growth. Make minor adjustments, like repositioning ventilation panels or adding a small fan to circulate air. Not only does this prevent mold growth, but it also helps maintain a stable environment for your pet. If pests are the problem, consider introducing natural pest control methods. Beneficial insects, such as predatory mites, can be your allies, keeping unwanted bugs at bay without harming your pet. You might even find that certain microfauna can help maintain the balance, acting as gatekeepers for your bioactive community and keeping the riffraff out while letting the A-listers stay.

Recognizing the early signs of habitat issues is crucial to addressing problems promptly. Pay attention to the substrate—discoloration or foul odors can signal trouble. If your pet starts displaying abnormal behaviors, such as excessive hiding or unusual aggression, it may be trying to tell you that something is amiss in its environment. These subtle hints are your pet's way of waving a tiny flag that says, "Hey, something's not right here!" Regularly inspect the enclosure for signs of wear and tear, as well as any malfunctioning equipment. A faulty heater or light could lead to more significant issues, so it's best to catch these early.

Proactively managing your pet's habitat is like being a vigilant landlord, constantly ensuring everything is in top shape for your tenant. Routine inspections of equipment functionality can prevent minor hiccups from becoming major headaches. Regular updates to the habitat design can optimize conditions, ensuring your pet's environment remains ideal and adaptable to its growing needs. Think of it as a little home makeover now and then, keeping things fresh and functional with no need of a reality TV crew.

Paying attention and acting quickly can stop slight problems from becoming big ones. Regular checks and adjustments help maintain a healthy and safe environment for your pet, allowing it to thrive in its little kingdom. These minor efforts can make a big difference, ensuring that both you and your pet enjoy a harmonious living situation. As you continue to monitor and improve your pet's habitat, you'll find that these troubleshooting skills become second nature, making you not just a pet owner but a habitat whisperer.

With your habitat challenges under control, it's time to look forward to the next chapter, where we'll explore how nutrition and feeding play a crucial role in your pet's well-being. From crafting balanced meal plans to understanding your companion's dietary needs, we'll delve into the world of exotic pet cuisine, ensuring your pet stays healthy and happy.

Troubleshooting Habitat Problems

Even with the best setup, issues may still arise. Here's how to fix them:

1. Problem: My pet seems too hot!

- Signs: Open-mouth breathing, excessive hiding, and avoidance of the heat lamp.

- Solution: Lower the temperature using a thermostat, adjust the basking light height, or provide more shade.

2. Problem: My pet isn't shedding correctly.

- Signs: Retained skin, dull coloration, dry patches.

- Solution: Increase humidity, mist enclosure, and add a rough-textured hide for rubbing.

3. Mold is growing in the enclosure!
   - Signs: White or green fuzzy patches on substrate or decorations.

   - Solution: Improve ventilation, reduce misting frequency, and promptly remove affected areas.

4. Problem: My plants keep dying!
   - Signs: Yellowing leaves, mold, wilting.

   - Solution: Adjust light exposure, use the correct soil type, and ensure humidity matches plant needs.

5. Quick Fixes:
   - Move the enclosure away from direct sunlight or drafts.

   - Adjust ventilation to control humidity.

   - Ensure the substrate stays clean and replace as needed.

Chapter 3: Nutrition and Feeding

What to Feed, When to Feed, and Why it Matters

I magine your exotic pet as a tiny, scaly gourmand wandering through the culinary landscape of its habitat. Whether munching on a leafy buffet or catching the latest cricket match, what you feed your exotic pet is as crucial as the air it breathes. The proper diet keeps your pet healthy and reveals the vibrant personality beneath those scales or feathers. Each species has its own unique dietary needs, and understanding these requirements is crucial to a happy and thriving pet. This chapter will reveal the secrets of feeding your exotic companions, ensuring they live a long, fulfilling life.

Let's dive into the world of herbivores, where iguanas and tortoises reign supremely. These leafy green enthusiasts are the vegans of the reptile world, noshing on a diet primarily composed of fresh greens. According to the experts at VCA Hospitals, an iguana's diet should consist of 80%-90% dark green, leafy vegetables, such as collard greens or mustard greens, with the remaining 10%-20% reserved for fruits and edible flowers. These pets are hindgut fermenters, which means they rely on gut microbes to break down fiber, making a plant-based diet not just preferred but essential. For tortoises, a similar approach applies, emphasizing variety to ensure they receive all necessary nutrients. Overlook their dietary needs, and you might find your iguana developing health issues faster than you can say "kale salad."

Meanwhile, in the insectivore corner, we have the geckos and chameleons, who prefer their meals with a side of wriggle. These critters thrive on a diet rich in insects, such as crickets and mealworms, which they hunt with the precision of a ninja. However, beware that store-bought crickets can lack essential nutrients, potentially leading to deficiencies in trace minerals and vitamins, as noted in various reptile nutrition studies. To combat this, "gut-loading" your insects before feeding them to your pet can ensure they pack a nutritional punch. This involves feeding the insects a nutrient-rich diet 24 hours before they become dinner, transforming them into little protein powerhouses.

Diet affects more than just the waistline; it influences behavior and overall health. Nutritional deficiencies can lead to serious health issues, from weak bones to lethargy, which is why it's crucial to balance the diet correctly. For instance, a calcium deficit in reptiles can cause metabolic bone disease, a condition as dire as it sounds. Dietary imbalances can trigger behavioral changes. A chameleon that is not getting enough nutrients might become irritable or lethargic, while an iguana with too much fruit in its diet could become as hyper as a child on Halloween. The key is to provide a balanced diet that meets all their nutritional needs, ensuring they remain in optimal health and vitality.

Finding the correct dietary information can feel like searching for a needle in a haystack. But fear not! Reliable resources are available to guide you on this culinary journey. Consulting with exotic pet nutritionists is a wise move, as they offer personalized advice tailored to your pet's specific needs. They can help you navigate the world of supplements and dietary adjustments, ensuring your pet gets the proper nutrients. Reputable websites and scientific journals also provide valuable insights. They're like the food critics of the exotic pet world, offering reviews and recommendations for the best dietary practices.

Adapting diets to individual pets is as important as tailoring a suit to fit. No two pets are alike, and factors such as age, activity level, and personal preferences can influence their dietary needs. A young iguana might require more protein for growth. Adults may benefit from a calcium-rich diet to maintain bone health, as suggested by various studies on reptile nutrition. Monitoring your pet's dietary responses and making adjustments as needed ensures that it continues to thrive. Monitor their weight, energy levels, and overall behavior, as these can provide clues about how well the current diet is working. If your chameleon turns its nose up at crickets, it might be time to introduce a variety or consult with a vet.

Crafting Balanced Meal Plans: Frequency and Portion Sizes

Creating a balanced meal plan for your exotic pet is akin to crafting a well-curated playlist—each element needs to hit the right note. The foundation of a good diet involves combining proteins, fats, and carbohydrates in the proper proportions. This means incorporating fresh fruits and vegetables to complement the mix for omnivores. Think of your pet as a discerning diner at a buffet, where each item on the plate plays a crucial role in their nutrition. Proteins are the primary course, providing building blocks for muscles and tissues, while fats serve as a concentrated energy source. Though sometimes sidelined, carbohydrates are essential for energy, particularly for active species. Fresh fruits and veggies add those vital vitamins and minerals that keep everything ticking smoothly, like the final garnish on a gourmet dish.

The frequency and size of meals are just as crucial as the ingredients themselves. Small reptiles, for instance, benefit from daily feeding schedules. They have fast metabolisms and need regular nutrient intake to maintain energy levels. Picture them as tiny athletes who need their daily energy bars to keep going. Meanwhile, nocturnal feeders might enjoy larger meals spread over fewer days, aligning with their natural feeding patterns. It's like setting the dining room table for dinner, with each chair (or meal) representing a different day. Timing and portion sizes significantly affect your pet's health. Excessive food intake can lead to obesity, a common issue in captive animals, while insufficient food intake can cause nutrient deficiencies, leaving them feeling as though they've missed breakfast.

Accurate portion sizes are vital to avoid overfeeding or underfeeding. Using digital scales helps ensure precise measurements, giving you a clear picture of how much food your pet needs. Think of it as using a measuring cup when baking—accuracy prevents disaster.

Visual guides can also help estimate portion sizes, especially when scales aren't handy. This method involves comparing food amounts to familiar objects, such as a deck of cards or a golf ball, to determine the correct portion size. It's all about finding that balance where your pet is left hungry or overwhelmed by their meal.

Common pitfalls in meal planning can trip up even the most diligent pet owner. Overfeeding might seem like a generous gesture, but it can lead to obesity, which is as detrimental to pets as it is to humans. Picture your pet waddling around like a fluffy ball—not ideal. Underfeeding can leave your pet malnourished, lacking the energy and nutrients necessary for optimal health and well-being. This can lead to various health issues, including poor growth and development, as well as a weakened immune system, making them more susceptible to illness. Nutrient deficiencies are like the villain in a superhero movie, quietly plotting to overthrow your pet's health.

Visual Element: Meal Planning Checklist

Keep your pet's diet on track with this simple checklist:

1. Balance: Are you combining proteins, fats, and carbohydrates in a balanced way?

2. Fruits & Veggies: Have you included fresh produce for your omnivore?

3. Frequency: Is your feeding schedule aligned with your pet's needs?

4. Portion Control: Using tools like scales or visual guides to measure portions?

5. Watch Out: Have you checked for signs of overfeeding or

underfeeding?

Following these guidelines and adjusting as needed ensures your exotic pet stays healthy and happy.

Safe and Unsafe Foods: Navigating Dietary Hazards

Imagine your exotic pet sitting at a table, a napkin tucked into its collar, ready to feast on a delicious spread. But wait! Not everything on this table is safe. Navigating the world of exotic pet diets is akin to walking through a culinary minefield. Some foods, like leafy greens for your herbivorous iguana or tortoise, are safe and beneficial. These greens, such as collard and dandelion greens, are rich in nutrients and should form the foundation of their diet. For insectivorous species like geckos and chameleons, crickets and mealworms provide the protein punch they need to thrive. These critters are like little nutrition, ensuring your pet gets the energy it needs for daily antics.

However, not all foods are created equally. Some common human foods can be downright dangerous for your exotic pets. Take avocados, for instance. While they might be the star of your toast, they are toxic to many exotic animals. Chocolate, too, is a no-go zone. It contains theobromine, which is poisonous to most animals, including our scaled and feathered friends. Beware of pesticide-laden produce. Many fruits and vegetables can carry harmful residues if ingested by your pet. Always wash produce thoroughly, or opt for organic options to minimize the risk of exposure to these toxic chemicals. It's about keeping their diet as clean as possible, much like you'd avoid mystery meat at the buffet.

Spotting food-related health issues can feel like deciphering a secret code. Your pet can't tell you it feels under the weather, but it can show you. Vomiting or diarrhea might be your first clue that something's amiss, possibly from ingesting something toxic. If your usually energetic pet suddenly turns lethargic, it might suffer from nutrient imbalances. Such symptoms are your pet's way of waving a red flag, signaling that its diet needs adjusting. These signs indicate that all is not well in its digestive world. Like a detective piecing together clues, you'll need to investigate its recent meals to identify the culprit and consult with a vet if symptoms persist.

When introducing new foods to your pet's diet, think of it as a culinary experiment. You wouldn't dive headfirst into an all-you-can-eat sushi buffet without trying a piece first, right? The same principle applies to your pet. Introduce new foods gradually, one at a time, and closely monitor how your pet reacts. This approach allows you to spot any adverse reactions or allergies before they become serious. It's like dipping your toes in the water before committing to a swim. Watching your pet during this period is key. Look for signs of discomfort, changes in behavior, or physical reactions such as skin irritations or digestive issues. These can all show that a particular food dislikes your pet.

In this world of exotic pet feeding, caution is your best friend. By understanding which foods are safe and which are hazardous, you can keep your pet healthy and happy. Like a savvy chef, you'll craft a diet that satisfies their nutritional needs and keeps them out of harm's way.

The Role of Supplements: Ensuring Nutritional Balance

Imagine your reptile as a tiny, scaly superhero, leaping tall crickets in a single bound. But even superheroes need a little help now and then, which is where dietary supplements come into play. For many exotic pets, particularly reptiles, supplements are the sidekicks that ensure they get all the nutrients they need. Calcium supplements are especially crucial for reptiles to prevent metabolic bone disease, a rather nasty condition can weaken their bones faster than kryptonite. Since many reptiles don't get enough calcium from their diet alone, supplementing is essential to maintain their health. Meanwhile, vitamin D3 is another superhero in the world of supplements, especially for indoor pets that lack natural sunlight exposure. This vitamin helps with calcium absorption, making it a dynamic duo with calcium itself. Without the right amount of vitamin D3, your pet might as well be trying to sunbathe under a flashlight.

Choosing the right supplements can feel like trying to find the perfect avocado—not too hard, not too soft, and not too expensive. Evaluating supplement brands and ingredients is your first step. Look for reputable brands that provide transparent information about their products. Avoid anything that sounds like it belongs in a comic book rather than a pet store. Consulting with veterinarians can also guide you in selecting safe and effective products. They can recommend specific brands and formulations tailored to your pet's needs. Just like you wouldn't ask your dentist for advice on grooming your dog, trust the experts who know the ins and outs of exotic pet nutrition.

Incorporating supplements into your pet's diet requires a touch of culinary flair. Dusting insects with calcium powder is a standard method for reptiles, turning their dinner into a nutrient-rich feast. Imagine it as a light sprinkle of parmesan on your pasta—just enough to enhance the flavor without overwhelming it. For those pets that prefer their vitamins in liquid form, mixing them into water or food can be effective. Just follow the instructions carefully, as too much of a good thing can become terrible. Like when you thought more hot sauce would improve your chili—it didn't.

Over-supplementation is a real risk and monitoring dosages closely is essential. Excessive use of supplements can lead to toxicity, particularly with fat-soluble vitamins like A, D, E, and K. You don't want your pet turning into a vitamin overdose poster child. Monitor their health and behavior for any adverse effects, such as changes in appetite, energy levels, or physical appearance. These can be subtle hints that something isn't quite right. Monitoring and adjusting supplement intake as needed ensures your pet remains on the path to optimal health without straying into the realm of excessive supplementation.

Supplements are a valuable tool in maintaining your exotic pet's health, providing the nutrients they might not get from their diet alone. With the right balance, your pet can thrive, showing off their full superhero potential with no need for a cape.

Feeding Techniques: From Hand-feeding to Automated Systems

Feeding your exotic pet can be a delightful experience reminiscent of a culinary adventure. Whether you're offering treats by hand or relying on the wonders of technology, the method you choose can significantly affect your pet's health and your relationship with them. Hand-feeding is the gold standard for building a bond with your pet. When you offer food directly, you create opportunities for interaction and trust-building. Imagine a moment where you gently present a piece of fruit to your iguana, and it cautiously reaches out, acknowledging you as a friend. This simple act can reinforce the bond between you and your pet, making every meal an opportunity for connection. However, hand-feeding also requires time and patience. It's not always workable if you're juggling a hectic schedule, and some pets might prefer a more hands-off approach.

Enter the world of automated feeders, where convenience meets consistency. These gadgets can dispense food at regular intervals, freeing you from the tyranny of the clock. Imagine heading out for the day, confident that your pet's meals are taken care of without you needing to lift a finger. Automated feeders are beneficial for fish and reptiles, who benefit from routine feedings with no direct human interaction. These devices ensure your pet receives the right amount of food at the right time, reducing the risk of overfeeding or missing meals. However, they also come with their own set of challenges. For instance, some pets may miss the social interaction that Hand feeding provides, and there is always the risk of a mechanical malfunction, leaving your pet hungry if you don't keep a close eye on things.

As you navigate these feeding techniques, having the right tools can make all the difference. Tongs and tweezers are invaluable for feeding insects to your reptile friends. They keep your fingers safe from curious bites and allow precise placement of prey, reducing mess and ensuring your pet gets the meal, not the substrate. For aquatic pets, automated fish feeders are a significant change. These devices distribute flakes, pellets, or even live food, ensuring your fish stays well-fed while you focus on other tasks. Selecting the right equipment involves considering the specific needs of your pet and the practicality of the tool in your daily routine. It's like choosing the proper kitchen utensils—each has its purpose, and using the wrong one can end in disaster (or at least a very messy meal).

Interactive feeding can transform mealtime into a stimulating activity, engaging your pet's instincts and mental faculties. Think of it like a puzzle for their brain, where they need to work a little to get their reward. Puzzle feeders, for example, encourage natural foraging behaviors, allowing pets to engage with their environment meaningfully. These feeders can vary in complexity, ranging from simple designs that require a gentle nudge to release food, to intricate mazes that challenge even the cleverest critters. Engaging feeding practices not only provide mental stimulation but also reduce boredom, potentially preventing destructive behaviors that arise from idle paws or claws. A chameleon might enjoy a game of hide-and-seek with its crickets, while a parrot might relish solving a puzzle to access seeds.

But what happens when your pet turns its nose up at dinner? Feeding challenges can arise, leaving you puzzled and your pet peckish. Addressing refusal to eat can be as simple as introducing variety into their diet. Just as you might tire of the same meal every day, your pet might crave something different. Offering a range of food options can rekindle their interest in mealtime. Maintaining hygiene and cleanliness in feeding areas is crucial. Dirty dishes can deter even the hungriest reptile, much like a sticky restaurant table might deter you. Regular cleaning of feeding areas and equipment helps prevent the buildup of bacteria, ensuring your pet's dining experience is pleasant and safe.

Feeding your exotic pet is more than just a routine task; it's an opportunity to connect, enrich, and ensure their well-being. Whether your hand-feeding or relying on automated systems, each method has its place in the world of exotic pets. By selecting the right tools and techniques, you can establish a feeding routine that suits both you and your pet, making every meal a moment of joy and discovery.

Addressing Dietary Challenges: Appetite Loss and Picky Eaters

Imagine waking up one day to find your usually voracious iguana has turned its nose up at breakfast. What gives? Appetite loss and selective eating are common dietary challenges in exotic pets, often leaving owners at a loss. Stress is a significant factor, with environmental changes playing a mischievous role. A move, a new pet in the house, or even a change in furniture arrangement can disrupt your pet's sense of balance. It's like switching your favorite coffee shop—suddenly, nothing tastes quite right. Illness or discomfort can also lead to a refusal to eat. If your pet seems off its game, it might be time to check for underlying health issues. A vet visit can help rule out medical concerns, ensuring your pet isn't dealing with something more serious than a case of the picky-eater blues.

So, how do you tempt a reluctant eater back to the table? Start by rotating food items to keep things interesting. Even the most steadfast of iguanas can tire of the same leafy greens day in and day out. Introducing variety can rekindle their interest in food, much like adding a new dish to your weekly dinner rotation. Enhancing palatability with natural flavors is another trick. A dash of fruit juice or a sprinkle of calcium powder can transform an ordinary meal into a gourmet experience. It's akin to adding a pinch of salt to your cooking. Suddenly, the flavors pop. These tweaks can make a world of difference in enticing your pet to eat, turning each meal into an expected event rather than a dreaded chore.

Monitoring and addressing underlying issues are crucial for long-term success. Regular health check-ups can rule out illnesses that might be affecting your pet's appetite. Think of it as a wellness visit to ensure everything is running smoothly. Behavioral assessments can also help identify stress-related eating issues. Perhaps your iguana isn't just picky, but is reacting to a change in its environment. Understanding these factors allows you to adjust, offering a more harmonious living space. This proactive approach helps ensure your pet remains healthy and content, reducing the likelihood of recurring appetite issues.

Sharing stories and techniques from experienced owners can offer valuable insights. Consider the tale of a chameleon that refused crickets for weeks. After much trial and error, its owner discovered that gradually introducing new foods worked wonders. Mixing its favorite mealworms with the less favored crickets, they slowly transitioned the pet to a more balanced diet. Another pet owner found success using favorite foods as incentives. They encouraged a reluctant gecko to expand its palate by incorporating beloved treats into meals. These anecdotes highlight the importance of patience and creativity in overcoming dietary challenges, proving persistence pays off.

In the grand scheme, addressing dietary challenges is about understanding your pet's unique needs and preferences. With some patience and culinary creativity, you can ensure your exotic pet receives a balanced diet, maintaining its health and vitality. As we wrap up our culinary exploration, remember that nutrition is a cornerstone of your pet's well-being, influencing everything from energy levels to behavior. With the right approach, you can transform mealtime into an opportunity for connection and care, fostering a deeper bond with your exotic companion.

As we conclude our deep dive into exotic pet nutrition, remember that a well-fed pet is a happy pet. With the right balance of nutrients and a sprinkle of love, your pet will thrive, delighting you with its antics and charm. Next, we'll explore the world of health and veterinary care, ensuring your pet remains in peak condition for all the adventures ahead.

Chapter 4: Health and Veterinary Care

Preventative care your pet will live a longer, healthier life.

Imagine you're at a bustling street fair, surrounded by the vibrant sounds of laughter and the enticing aroma of funnel cakes. You're having the time of your life when you notice your iguana—your trusty sidekick—looking sluggish in its carrier. Before panicking and spilling your lemonade, take a deep breath. Recognizing when your exotic buddy isn't feeling their best isn't just important; it's your key to becoming the superhero they need. Exotic pets, in their mysterious ways, often hide symptoms of illness. They took an oath of secrecy, making early detection a challenge even for the most attentive owner.

But fear not, for this chapter serves as your guide to deciphering the subtle signals your pet may send your way.

Let's start with the basics. Just as you might feel a bit off after a weekend of binge-watching and eating pizza, exotic pets can exhibit signs of illness through changes in their behavior. When your once-bouncy ferret turns into a couch potato, it's time to take note. Lethargy and inactivity are red flags waving in the wind, signaling that something might be amiss. Similarly, if your snake, who gobbles up its dinner with gusto, starts refusing meals, pay attention. Changes in eating habits or unexpected weight loss could be your pet's way of saying, "Hey, something's not right here!" These subtle shifts in behavior are often the first signs that your pet may not be feeling its best. Spotting these signs early can make all the difference in preventing a minor issue from snowballing into a major health crisis.

Early detection is your most powerful tool in the fight against illness. It's like catching a plot twist in your favorite mystery novel before anyone else. When you notice any unusual symptoms, prompt veterinary consultation is crucial. Exotic pets have a tendency to decline rapidly if not treated in a timely manner, so don't delay. Think of your vet as the detective who can piece together the clues your pet is leaving. Regularly recording your pet's health helps you monitor their behavior and physical state. This simple habit can be a lifesaver, offering a comprehensive view of your pet's health. Note their eating habits, activity levels, and any other notable quirks you may observe. This log becomes an invaluable resource for your vet, providing insights that might not be apparent during a quick office visit.

Observing and documenting symptoms is like being a wildlife photographer, capturing those fleeting moments that reveal so much.

Create a symptom checklist for common ailments your pet might face, such as respiratory issues or changes in fecal output. Checkboxes are your friends here, providing a quick reference to ensure nothing slips through the cracks. Photo documentation is another tool in your arsenal. A picture of that unusual swelling or discoloration can speak volumes to your vet, offering a visual record of changes. This photographic evidence helps track the progression of symptoms and helps diagnose the issue accurately.

Familiarity with your pet's normal behavior is the foundation of successful health monitoring. Regular interaction and observation allow you to establish a baseline for what's typical and what's not. Spend time each day observing your pet's activity levels and feeding patterns. When something deviates from the norm, you'll be the first to notice. Consider it akin to knowing your favorite song by heart—the moment a note goes awry, you know something's off. This understanding equips you to act swiftly, ensuring your pet receives the care it needs without delay. By staying attuned to your pet's everyday antics, you'll be better prepared to spot the subtle signs of illness that might otherwise go unnoticed.

Interactive Element: Health Monitoring Checklist

- Keep track of your pet's health with this easy-to-use checklist:

- Behavior Changes: Have you noticed any lethargy or unusual activity?

- Eating Habits: Is your pet eating less or showing disinterest in food?

- Physical Symptoms: Are there any visible changes, such as swelling or discoloration?

- Weight: Has there been any unexpected weight loss or gain?

- Respiratory Signs: Is your pet showing signs of labored breathing or wheezing?

- Fecal Output: Are there changes in consistency or frequency?

By diligently observing and documenting your pet's health, you become their best advocate, ensuring they receive the care and attention they deserve. Remember, every minor detail can be a clue in the bigger picture of your pet's well-being.

Preventive Health Measures: Vaccinations and Regular Check-Ups

Imagine your exotic pet as a tiny explorer setting out on its daily adventures around your home. Whether it's your parrot practicing its stand-up routine or your turtle trying to blend in with the garden gnomes, they all share one thing in common: the need for preventive health measures to keep their explorations safe and sound. Vaccinations play a critical role in this health maintenance, acting as invisible shields that protect against various diseases. Each species has its own set of vaccine recommendations, much like a personalized health plan. For our feathered friends, vaccinations against polyoma or avian influenza are crucial, especially if they're the life of the party among other birds. Rabbits may need vaccines for myxomatosis and RHDV2, which sound like alien invaders but are actually serious diseases that require attention. Understanding the timing of these vaccines, including when boosters are necessary, is akin to knowing when to change the oil in your car—it keeps things running smoothly.

But vaccinations are just one piece of the puzzle. Regular veterinary check-ups are the cornerstone of a healthy pet life. Think of these as wellness exams, like your yearly physical; your vet evaluates your pet's overall health during these exams. These annual examinations are vital for catching potential issues before they become big, hairy problems. During these visits, your vet might check growth and developmental milestones, ensuring your bearded dragon isn't suddenly sprouting wings or your hamster isn't auditioning for a part in a horror movie. Regular check-ups allow your vet to monitor your pet's health over time, making it easier to spot any deviations from their normal patterns. This proactive approach can lead to early intervention, preventing minor concerns from escalating into major health crises.

Incorporating preventive care routines into your pet's life is like setting a foundation for their health. Daily practices, such as grooming and hygiene checks, keep your exotic companion looking their best and feeling even better. This can mean brushing your rabbit's fur to prevent matting or providing a humid hide for your snake to help with shedding. Monthly, evaluate your pet's environment, looking for ways to enrich their habitat and support mental health. Adding new toys, changing the layout of their enclosure, or even introducing a new climbing branch can stimulate their minds and keep them engaged. Environmental enrichment is not just about avoiding boredom; it's about encouraging natural behaviors that contribute to overall well-being.

The benefits of preventive care extend beyond the immediate. Taking these steps beforehand will help your pet live longer and healthier. By reducing the risk of common diseases, you're essentially giving your pet a head start in the race against time. Preventive care enhances the quality of life, allowing your pet to enjoy the simple pleasures—like a sunbeam nap or a good scratch behind the ears—without the looming cloud of illness. It's like having a safety net, ensuring that even if life throws a curveball, your pet is prepared to catch it with grace. Regular care routines, paired with the watchful eye of a vet, create a wellness plan that supports your pet through each stage of life.

Maintaining your exotic pet's health is a multifaceted endeavor that requires attention to detail and a commitment to their well-being. By embracing vaccinations, regular check-ups, and preventive routines, you're not just caring for an animal; you're fostering a vibrant and fulfilling life for a cherished companion. Whether they're scaling their terrarium walls or serenading you with their melodious chirps, a healthy pet is a happy pet, ready to share their world with you in ways you might never have imagined.

Finding and Working with Exotic Pet Veterinarians

Finding a veterinarian who truly understands the quirks and needs of exotic pets can feel like hunting for buried treasure. Your iguana doesn't just need any vet; it needs one who speaks the language of scales and tails. Start your search with online directories dedicated to exotic pet vets. These are like matchmaking sites, but instead of finding love, you're finding the perfect health care provider for your pet. Sites like the Association of Avian Veterinarians or the Association of Exotic Mammal Veterinarians offer lists of specialists in your area. Local pet owner groups can also be goldmines for recommendations. These are experienced people who can share their knowledge and guide you. Dolittle of the exotic pet world.

When evaluating potential vets, you'll want to consider several factors to ensure a good fit for your pet's needs. Experience with specific exotic species is crucial. A vet who has successfully treated a bearded dragon's skin infection or a parrot's dietary issue is worth their weight in gold. Client testimonials and reviews can provide insight into the vet's reputation and the quality of care they provide. Look for feedback that mentions positive outcomes and a compassionate approach. You want a vet who doesn't just see your pet as a number but as a unique individual with its own set of needs and challenges. A good vet should also be up-to-date with the latest research and techniques in exotic pet care, ensuring your pet receives the best possible treatment.

Establishing a strong relationship with your chosen vet is like forming a partnership, with your pet's health as the goal. Start by preparing detailed health histories for vet visits. This includes any previous illnesses, dietary preferences, and any quirks your pet might have, such as its inexplicable fear of the color yellow. These details can provide a valuable context for the vet, helping them tailor their approach to your pet's specific situation. Don't be afraid to ask questions and seek clarification on care advice. As a pet owner, it's your right to understand the treatment plan and any procedures your pet may undergo. Building trust with your vet involves open communication and a willingness to collaborate on your pet's care.

To make the most of veterinary appointments, a little preparation goes a long way. Before the visit, jot down questions or concerns you might have about your pet's health. This ensures you cover all your bases and don't leave the clinic with that nagging feeling of forgetting something important. During the appointment, take notes on the advice and treatment plans provided by the vet. This helps you remember the details and allows you to refer to them later. You may also want to consider bringing a notebook or using a note-taking app on your phone to keep everything organized. Having a record of discussions and recommendations can be invaluable, especially if you need to follow up on specific treatments or monitor your pet's progress.

Your relationship with your exotic vet is a vital component of your pet's well-being. With the right vet, you'll have a trusted partner to navigate the difficulties of exotic pet ownership, ensuring your furry, scaly, or feathery friend receives the best care possible. Finding that perfect vet might take time, but once you do, you'll have peace of mind knowing your pet is in capable hands.

Common Health Problems: Symptoms and Treatments

Picture this: you're observing your reptile friend basking under its heat lamp. Suddenly, you notice a little more than the usual snooze-induced lethargy. Your gecko seems to wheeze, its breath coming in sharp little gasps. Respiratory infections are a common woe for reptiles, often stemming from inadequate humidity or temperature swings more erratic than a soap opera plot twist. You'll want to keep an eye out for signs like labored breathing, nasal discharge, or a noticeable lack of interest in that cricket buffet you laid out with love. These symptoms can escalate quickly, so it's time to play detective and consider a visit to the vet if you suspect an infection is afoot.

Amphibians face their own set of challenges. Parasite infestations can wreak havoc on these slippery critters, leading to weight loss, skin abnormalities, or even a reluctance to soak up water. Parasites are like the uninvited guests at a party; they show up, eat all the snacks, and leave chaos in their wake. Spotting the signs early is crucial. Look for changes in behavior or unexplained weight fluctuations. If your frog seems more aloof than usual or your salamander is shedding skin like it's going out of style, it might be time to probe further. A vet can perform diagnostic tests, such as fecal exams or blood work, to identify the pesky invaders and prescribe the right course of treatment.

Diagnosis is where science meets sleuthing. Veterinarians may use laboratory tests or imaging to pinpoint the exact cause of an illness. It's like CSI, but with geckos and guinea pigs. Behavioral indicators also provide valuable clues. An exotic pet that's suddenly more high-strung than your morning coffee might try to tell you something isn't right. Accurate diagnosis is the key to effective treatment; therefore, providing your veterinarian with as much information as possible can make all the difference. After identifying the root cause, your veterinarian will recommend treatment options, which may include medication or adjustments to your pet's care regimen.

With treatment, there are several options available. Prescription medications often form the cornerstone of addressing health issues. Administering these meds might feel daunting at first, like trying to convince a toddler to eat their veggies. But with a bit of practice, you'll find a routine that works for both you and your pet. Supportive care at home also plays a significant role in recovery. This could involve adjusting your pet's habitat to optimize its comfort and promote healing. You may need to change the humidity levels, provide additional warmth, or offer a special diet to support recovery. These minor adjustments can create a more conducive environment for your pet's recuperation.

Follow-up care is just as critical as the initial treatment. It's like baking a cake—you wouldn't stop halfway through, would you? Monitoring your pet's progress is crucial to ensure a full recovery. Schedule follow-up visits with your vet to assess how the treatment works and make any necessary adjustments. Your pet might need a different course of medication or further tests to confirm they're back to their usual mischievous self. During recovery, you may also need to change their diet or habitat, ensuring they have everything they need to bounce back stronger than ever. Keep a close eye on any lingering symptoms and don't hesitate to contact your veterinarian if you have concerns. With the right care and attention, your exotic friend can enjoy a healthy, thriving life once more.

Emergency Care: What to Do in Critical Situations

Imagine it's a typical Tuesday evening. You're kicking back, binge-watching your favorite show with your exotic pet snug nearby when, suddenly, the unthinkable happens. Your parrot wheezes, or your snake seems to have swallowed something suspicious. It's an exotic pet owner's nightmare, but staying calm is your first line of defense. Recognizing life-threatening symptoms is crucial. Watch for signs like rapid breathing, bleeding, or unconsciousness. These are your pet's SOS signals, showing that something is seriously wrong. As soon as you notice any of these signs, contact emergency veterinary services immediately. Keep your vet's number on speed dial and know the location of the nearest emergency clinic. Time is often of the essence in emergencies, and acting quickly can make all the difference.

Being prepared for such scenarios means having an emergency kit ready to go. Think of it as your pet's personal first-aid kit, stocked with essentials that can stabilize them until professional help arrives. Include antiseptics to clean wounds and bandages to control bleeding. Tweezers can be handy for removing small foreign objects, while a digital thermometer helps monitor your pet's temperature. Don't forget an emergency contact list for your vet and specialists, ensuring you have all the numbers you need at your fingertips. Having this kit accessible is like having a safety net; it's there to catch you when things go sideways, giving you the tools to provide immediate care.

Let's talk about common emergencies and how to handle them. If your pet starts choking or swallows something suspicious, first ensure they're still breathing. For birds, gently open their beak and remove any visible blockages. For reptiles, a gentle massage of the throat may help dislodge small objects. Be cautious not to push the item further down. In cases of physical injury, such as a broken limb, immobilize the area with a bandage or splint to reduce movement until you can get to the vet. For cuts or abrasions, clean the area with antiseptic and apply gauze to prevent infection. Remember, your goal is to stabilize your pet, not perform surgery in your living room. Seek professional help as soon as possible to ensure proper treatment.

Remaining calm and organized during these moments is easier said than done. Practicing emergency drills with family members can help everyone stay calm when the actual situation arises. Assign roles, such as who will gather the emergency kit or contact the vet, so everyone knows what to do. Keep emergency resources, such as your kit and contact list, in a designated, easily accessible spot. This organization minimizes panic and ensures you can act swiftly. In the heat of the moment, clear thinking prevails. Take a deep breath, assess the situation, and follow the steps you've practiced. Your pet depends on you to be their rock in times of crisis, and with preparation, you can rise to the occasion.

Building a Health Record: Tracking Medical History and Care

Picture this: Your iguana, affectionately named Spike, has been your scaly roommate for years. Spike has had his fair share of vet visits; from the time he snacked on a houseplant (oops) to his routine check-ups. Now, imagine needing to recall every detail of those visits from memory. It sounds like a nightmare, right? That's why keeping a comprehensive health record for your exotic pet is as crucial as keeping track of your medical history. A detailed log not only tracks vaccination dates and types, such as the herpes virus shot Spike received last summer, but also documents past illnesses and treatments. This meticulous record-keeping becomes a treasure trove of information, ensuring you're always prepared to share your pet's health journey with a new vet or when an emergency arises.

Organizing all this information might sound like a task suited for an accountant, but fear not. There are practical tools to help you stay on top of things. Printable health record templates are a significant starting point. They're like coloring books for adults, but with more purpose and less glitter. You can jot down all the vital stats, from vaccination schedules to dietary preferences. If paper isn't your thing, digital apps for tracking pet health data offer a high-tech alternative. These apps are handy for setting reminders, storing medical documents, and even scheduling alerts for upcoming vaccinations. They're essentially your pet's personal assistant, minus the coffee runs.

So, why go through all this effort? Thorough medical records can be your pet's best defense in future care. When Spike decides he's not feeling too hot and you rush him to the vet, having a complete history at your fingertips facilitates an accurate diagnosis. It's like handing the vet a map instead of asking them to navigate a maze blindfolded. These records streamline communication, especially when introducing a new veterinarian into the mix. No more fumbling through your phone to find old emails or trying to recall the name of that mysterious ailment Spike had two summers ago. This neatly compiled information makes the vet's job easier and Spike's care more efficient.

Regular updates and reviews of your pet's health records are the key benefit to keeping everything accurate and current. Set reminders for updating vaccination statuses, so you're not surprised when your vet asks about Spike's last booster shot. Periodically review these records with your veterinarian. Think of it as a coffee date but with fewer lattes and more discussions about reptile health. These check-ins ensure nothing slips through the cracks, and they can highlight any trends or changes in your pet's health that might need addressing. Staying on top of these updates not only keeps you informed but also shows your commitment to your pet's well-being.

As this chapter closes, remember that maintaining a detailed health record is like giving your pet an extra layer of care. It's not just about numbers and dates; it's about understanding and documenting their life with you. These records play a vital role in ensuring your pet receives the best possible care, now and in the future. With the right tools and a bit of diligence, you can become the record-keeping superhero of your pet needs, ready to tackle any health challenge that comes your way. As we move forward, we'll explore the fascinating world of handling and socialization, ensuring your exotic companion remains not just healthy, but also happy and well-adjusted.

Chapter 5: Handling and Socialization

Building Bonds Through Trust, Respect, and Routine

A h, handling your exotic pet—it's the moment you've been waiting for, like finally meeting your favorite celebrity, but with a few more scales and a lot fewer paparazzi. The first interaction can be a bit nerve-wracking for both you and your exotic companion. Picture this: you're reaching out to your pet, and it's looking at you like you're about to offer it a lifetime supply of crickets. However, don't worry - with the proper techniques, you'll become the dynamic duo of the pet world in no time.

Safe Handling Techniques: Building Confidence with Your Pet

Handling exotic pets isn't just about picking them up; it's an art form, much like attempting to eat spaghetti gracefully. Each species has its handling requirements and understanding these is crucial to avoid any unintended squirming or, worse, a defensive tail slap. For starters, use slow, deliberate movements. Imagine you're moving through a field of butterflies. Fast, erratic actions can startle your pet, making them feel like they're in the middle of an impromptu earthquake drill. Supporting your reptile's body correctly is also key. For snakes, this means helping their entire length, while lizards appreciate being held securely around their midsection, avoiding any Houdini-like escapes.

Introducing your pet to handling should be a gradual process, much like easing into a hot bath. Start with brief, gentle interactions, allowing your pet to become accustomed to your presence. Think of it as the "getting to know you" phase. Use treats as positive reinforce-ment—because who doesn't appreciate a little snack as a reward? According to Animal Care Unlimited, short periods of careful handling can help build trust, provided your pet doesn't feel threatened. With patience and consistency, your pet will soon associate your touch with positive experiences, rather than a surprise game of tag.

With handling tools, think safety first. Handling gloves can be a lifesaver—literally—offering protection from bites. These aren't your garden-variety gloves; they're designed to withstand the occasional nip without sacrificing your fingers. For larger reptiles, nets or hooks can be invaluable. They allow you to manage your pet confidently without causing undue stress. Picture yourself as a skilled animal wrangler, using the right equipment to ensure both you and your pet remain calm and collected. It's all about making handling a safe and enjoyable experience for everyone involved.

Observing your pet's behavior during handling is like having a conversation without words. Exotic pets communicate through body language and vocalizations, and learning to recognize these cues is crucial. If your pet puffs up, hiss, or make a sudden move, it's their way of saying, "I'm not in the mood right now!" note these signs and adjust your handling techniques accordingly. It's about finding that sweet spot where both you and your pet feel comfortable and secure. Adjusting your approach based on feedback can turn handling from a potential wrestling match into a harmonious, confidence-building routine.

Interactive Element: Handling Checklist

Use this checklist to ensure safe and effective handling:

- Movement: Are you using slow, deliberate actions?

- Support: Is your pet's body supported properly?

- Acclimation: Are you starting with brief interactions?

- Equipment: Do you have gloves or hooks ready if needed?

- Behavior: Are you observing and adjusting based on pet signals?

In this way, handling becomes a bridge to deeper connection, allowing you to bond with your pet while ensuring its comfort and safety.

Socialization Strategies: Encouraging Positive Interactions

Socialization for exotic pets works wonders for their mental health and behavior, a bit like a spa day for the soul. Imagine your pet as a social butterfly, fluttering around, curious and engaged with the world. When pets become familiar with their surroundings, anxiety melts away, leaving room for exploration and discovery. A well-socialized pet is more confident and content, making interactions smoother and more enjoyable for everyone involved. It's like watching a shy kid on the first day of school gradually transform into the class clown by semester's end. Familiarization with new environments encourages curiosity, allowing your pet to engage more fully with its surroundings and develop a richer, more fulfilling life.

To kick start the socialization process, you need to introduce your pet to new sights and sounds gradually. It's like gently dipping a toe into a pool versus cannon balling into the deep end. Start by letting your pet explore different rooms or spaces at their own pace, ensuring they feel secure and not overwhelmed. If you're introducing a parrot to a bustling household, begin with short, controlled visits to high-traffic areas, escalating the duration as they acclimate. For reptiles, you might play soft music or ambient sounds in the background, helping them get used to different auditory stimuli. Allowing pets to explore new areas independently builds their confidence, much like letting a toddler roam a playground under your watchful eye.

Positive reinforcement plays a crucial role in socialization, keeping the atmosphere light and encouraging. Think of it as giving your pet a gold star for good behavior. Offer food rewards when they remain calm in new situations. This helps them associate these experiences with positive outcomes. If your snake stays relaxed while exploring a new surface, reward it with a tasty treat. Clicker training can also be helpful, providing consistent cues that guide your pet's behavior. Each click signals a job well done, reinforcing desirable actions and helping your pet understand what's expected. This method is like a language, building a bridge of communication between you and your pet. Consistency is key, so reward the behaviors you want to see more of, encouraging your pet to repeat them.

Consider the success story of integrating a parrot into a lively home. Initially, the bird was overwhelmed by the noise and activity. By introducing it to the hustle and bustle gradually, and rewarding it for staying calm, the parrot soon adapted, even joining in with the odd whistle or mimicry of family members. Another instance involves a shy gecko, wary of human interaction. With patient exposure and gentle handling, this gecko transformed from a reclusive wallflower into a curious explorer, happy to perch on its owner's shoulder as they went about their day. These examples illustrate that with patience and the right approach, socialization can transform even the most timid pet into a confident companion.

Socialization is a rewarding experience for both you and your pet, fostering a deeper connection and mutual understanding. As you embark on this journey, remember that every pet is unique, and what works for one might not work for another. Stay patient, be consistent, and enjoy watching your exotic friend blossom into a well-adjusted member of your household.

Overcoming Fear: Addressing Common Handling Dilemmas

Handling an exotic pet for the first time can feel like defusing a bomb—you're not sure which wire to cut, and you're hoping it doesn't blow up in your face. The fear of being bitten or scratched is a common concern for new pet owners, and nobody enjoys a surprise nip from a disgruntled gecko. This fear isn't exclusive to humans; exotic pets often feel anxious around humans too. Imagine being picked up by a giant alien creature without warning—it's enough to make anyone a little jittery. Pets are often unfamiliar with human touch and may react defensively if startled. This anxiety can lead to tense interactions, making it crucial to approach handling with a strategy that's as much about building trust as it is about avoiding injury.

One effective way to tackle these handling fears is to practice with someone who knows the ropes. A calm, experienced handler can show you the ropes—or in this case, the scales and feathers. They can show gentle pet handling, offering tips to prevent those all-too-common mishaps. Gradual desensitization is another excellent method. Start by letting your pet get used to your presence. Spend time near their enclosure, allowing them to observe you without feeling threatened. Once they seem comfortable, you can introduce gentle handling, increasing the duration as your pet's comfort grows. Think of it as building a friendship over time—slow and steady wins the race. Each interaction should aim to build confidence, both yours and your pets, transforming fear into familiarity.

Patience is your best friend when handling exotic pets. It's like learning to play the guitar: you won't be a rock star overnight, and you might hit a few wrong notes along the way. Consistency is key to overcoming challenges. Establish a predictable routine, so your pet knows what to expect. This predictability reduces anxiety, allowing your pet to relax and trust the process. Celebrate small successes. Did your bearded dragon stay calm as you picked him up today? That's a win! Each positive interaction builds a foundation of trust, making the subsequent encounter that much smoother. Over time, these minor victories accumulate, creating a bond that makes handling a natural part of your relationship.

Even with the best-laid plans, every exotic pet owner will face unexpected reactions at some point. Perhaps your snake makes a sudden move, or your parrot takes flight with a startled squawk. In these moments, staying calm is vital. Take a deep breath and remain composed. Sudden flares of activity can be redirected by gently offering a toy or moving your pet's focus to something less threatening. Providing distractions not only shifts their attention but also helps diffuse the situation before it escalates. When your pet sees you as a steady, unflappable presence, it reinforces their trust in you. They begin to understand that you are predictable and safe, a source of comfort rather than fear.

Enrichment Activities: Stimulating Your Pet's Mind and Body

Imagine your exotic pet's enclosure as not just a home, but an interactive playground that caters to both their mental and physical well-being. Enrichment activities are the lifeblood of a vibrant, healthy environment, serving as the antidote to boredom and the key to unlocking your pet's natural instincts. Without a variety of engaging activities, even the most fascinating chameleon can become a couch potato, leading to destructive behaviors or, worse, a pet with the enthusiasm of a soggy noodle. You can keep your pet engaged and active by providing stimulating challenges that mimic the complexities of their natural habitat.

To create an environment that keeps your pet as engaged as a kid in a candy store, consider incorporating puzzle feeders and climbing structures. Puzzle feeders are effective for intellectual stimulation, turning mealtimes into exciting problem-solving sessions. These feeders can be as simple as a ball filled with treats or a more complex contraption that requires your pet to maneuver pieces to access their food. It's like giving your pet a Sudoku puzzle, except with a much tastier reward. Climbing structures cater to the physical needs of reptiles and birds, providing opportunities for exercise and exploration. These can range from branches and ropes to custom-built jungle gyms, encouraging your pet to stretch their limbs and satisfy their innate curiosity.

Using natural elements in enrichment activities can also significantly enhance engagement. Live plants are an excellent option, providing a lush landscape for exploration and even a snack for some herbivorous species. Introducing a few hardy plants like ferns or pothos can transform a barren enclosure into a thriving mini-ecosystem. Natural substrates such as sand or bark can also offer endless opportunities for digging and burrowing, allowing pets like tortoises or geckos to indulge in their favorite pastimes. Imagine your pet happily burrowing into a soft substrate, much like a child building sandcastle on the beach. These elements not only enrich your pet's environment but also create a more natural and appealing habitat.

Implementing these activities safely is crucial to ensure your pet's well-being. Monitor interactions with additional elements closely, much like a lifeguard at a pool party. This helps you catch any potential issues before they escalate. If your pet seems to get a bit too rowdy with a climbing structure or shows signs of stress around new plants, it might be time to adjust or remove these elements temporarily. Rotating toys and activities can also prevent boredom and maintain interest, ensuring your pet doesn't become too familiar or disinterested with their options. It's a bit like keeping a fresh playlist on your phone—variety keeps things exciting and engaging.

Visual Element: Enrichment Inspiration Chart

Use this chart to brainstorm and plan enrichment activities for your pet:

- Intellectual Stimulation: Puzzle feeders, foraging challenges

- Physical Exercise: Climbing structures, obstacle courses

- Natural Engagement: Live plants, digging substrates

- Safety Check: Monitor interactions, rotate activities

Incorporating these activities into your pet's daily routine can transform their world from a static enclosure to an ever-evolving landscape of discovery and delight. Your exotic friend will not only thrive, but may also surprise you with newfound behaviors and skills, revealing the depths of their complex and fascinating nature.

The Role of Routine: Establishing Consistent Interaction

Imagine waking up each morning to a routine that not only sets the tone for your day but also for your exotic pet's well-being. Just like us, pets thrive on consistency and predictability. Establishing a routine for your pet interactions can significantly reduce stress and foster trust. Think of it as setting their internal clock to "happy hour" at the same time every day. Consistent feeding and handling times become anchors in their daily lives. When your pet knows what to expect, it's less likely to experience anxiety. Morning feedings can be a gentle wake-up call, while evening handling sessions can serve as a cozy wind-down ritual. This rhythm creates a sense of security, making your pet more relaxed and open to interaction.

Creating a balanced interaction schedule is akin to planning a menu for a well-balanced diet. Both require thoughtfulness and attention to detail. Allocate specific times each day for handling and socialization, ensuring they become a natural part of your routine. This might mean setting aside time before work for a quick cuddle or dedicating a peaceful evening hour to bond over a shared activity. Balance is key, so remember to include rest periods in the mix. Just as you wouldn't want to run a marathon without a break, your pet needs downtime to recharge. This balance helps prevent overstimulation and ensures interactions remain positive and rewarding.

A consistent routine benefits both pets and owners by fostering a sense of security and predictability. Imagine your pet eagerly waiting at the same spot each day, anticipating the next interaction. This anticipation builds excitement and strengthens your bond. For you, it simplifies pet care and reduces stress, as you know exactly when and how to engage with your pet. Structured schedules also minimize anxiety, as your pet learns to trust the consistency of their environment. It's like having a favorite TV show that airs every Thursday night, something to look forward to that brings comfort and familiarity.

Consider the example of a morning feeding and evening handling ritual. Each day starts with a nutritious breakfast, setting a positive tone. In the evening, after the day's hustle and bustle, you spend time together, reinforcing your connection. This routine becomes a comforting cycle, deeply ingrained in your lives. Scheduled enrichment activities throughout the week add variety while maintaining a structured approach. Perhaps Monday is puzzle day, while Wednesday involves a new climbing challenge. These routines not only enhance your pet's quality of life but also deepen your understanding and appreciation of your exotic friend.

Through consistent routines, pet interactions transform from mere chores into meaningful rituals that enrich both your lives. As you establish these patterns, you'll notice a positive shift in your pet's behavior and your relationship. This harmonious balance becomes the foundation of your journey together, guiding you through the joys and challenges of owning an exotic pet.

Troubleshooting Behavioral Issues: Understanding Stress Signals

Even the most laid-back exotic pet can exhibit stress signals that might puzzle you more than a Rubik's Cube. Recognizing these signals is crucial because they are your pet's way of sending an SOS in a world that can sometimes feel overwhelming. You might notice your pet engaging in excessive hiding or avoidance behaviors, much like a child at a family reunion who would rather camp out under the table than mingle with distant relatives. Aggressive displays, such as hissing, biting, or flaring, are also standard. These aren't just dramatic moments worthy of a soap opera; they're clear indicators that your pet is feeling anxious or threatened. Vocalizations, though less common in some reptiles, can also be a sign. These behaviors are their way of saying, "Help, something's not right!"

Ignoring stress signals is akin to ignoring the low fuel warning on your car—eventually, it will lead to trouble. Prolonged stress can compromise your pet's immune function, making them more susceptible to illness. It's as if their body's defense system takes a vacation when you need it most. Chronic stress can also lead to behavioral shifts, turning a once docile pet into an aggressive one. You might find yourself facing a feisty bearded dragon that hurls itself at the enclosure's glass, or an ordinarily social parrot that suddenly refuses to leave its perch. These changes can strain your relationship with your pet, transforming what should be a joyful companionship into a challenge.

To mitigate stress, consider making adjustments to your pet's environment. Sometimes, it's as simple as rearranging a few elements to create a calming space, much like Feng shuiing your living room to promote tranquility. Ensure your pet has access to a cozy hideaway where it can retreat and feel secure. Introducing calming pheromones or scents is another option. These products mimic natural signals that can help soothe your pet, transforming their habitat into a serene sanctuary. The idea is to create an environment where your pet feels safe and relaxed, reducing the triggers that lead to stress. Minor changes can have a big impact, making your pet feel more at ease in its surroundings.

However, if stress signals persist despite your best efforts, it might be time to call in the pros. Consulting a behaviorist or veterinarian can provide insights and solutions tailored to your pet's needs, much like seeking a personal trainer to tackle a fitness plateau. Recognizing when stress signals show medical concerns is crucial. A behaviorist can help determine whether the issue is rooted in the environment, interactions, or health. Collaborating with these professionals can lead to a tailored behavior plan that addresses your pet's unique challenges. It's like getting a custom suit—it fits perfectly and addresses all the quirks that off-the-rack options cannot accommodate. Their expertise can guide you in making the adjustments, ensuring your pet's well-being and your peace of mind.

Understanding and addressing stress in your exotic pet is vital for maintaining a harmonious relationship. By paying attention to their signals and making thoughtful changes, you can create an environment where both you and your pet thrive. It's about finding that balance where life is a shared adventure, not a series of stressful encounters. As you continue to learn and adapt, remember that each step you take strengthens the bond you share with your exotic companion. Your pet relies on you to navigate these challenges, and with patience and care, you're well-equipped to do just that.

With handling and socialization under our belts, we move to the next chapter—caring for your pet's health and ensuring they thrive. Find out how to keep your exotic pet healthy.

Chapter 6 Legal and Ethical Considerations

Being an Informed and Responsible Exotic Pet Owner

P icture this: you've just brought home a charming little sugar glider. Its eyes are as big as saucers, and it's already won the hearts of everyone in your household. But before you know it, you're in a pickle because you didn't realize your town has a strict ban on owning such adorable creatures. You might think, "How could something so cute be illegal?" Welcome to the fascinating—and sometimes confusing—world of exotic pet laws. It's a realm where a lion might be a no-go, but a monkey gets the green light. Trust me, navigating these laws can feel like playing a round of bureaucratic bingo.

Let's explore why understanding local laws is crucial when it comes to owning exotic pets. The rules vary widely, not just from state to state, but also from city to city. Some places are stricter than a librarian during silent reading, while others are more lenient. For instance, South Carolina bans lions but not monkeys, which could lead to interesting neighborhood barbecue conversations. It's not just about knowing whether you can have that cute little critter; it's about understanding the legal implications that come with it. Think of it as learning the rules of a game before you play, so you know when you're in the clear and when you're in a heap of trouble. Familiarizing yourself with these laws is like having a GPS for the legal landscape, helping you avoid the potholes of non-compliance.

To get a grip on these regulations, you'll need to roll up your sleeves and do some research. Start by looking into your state's laws, which you can find on resources like FindLaw (Source 1). This will reveal which species are allowed and which are prohibited. But don't stop there! Dive deeper into municipal regulations, as local ordinances can add another layer of complexity. Zoning laws can also affect whether you're allowed to keep your exotic buddy in your home. It's like peeling an onion—each layer reveals more about the legal environment you're navigating. And just like onions, these laws can sometimes make you want to cry.

Now, if your dream pet requires a permit, here's a step-by-step guide to help you through the application maze. First, identify if your species of interest needs a permit. The requirements vary as much as the pets themselves, making this crucial. Next, gather all necessary documents, which might include proof of purchase, veterinary health reports, and a detailed plan of how you intend to care for your pet. Completing application forms accurately is essential. You don't want to miss a checkbox or misplace a signature—mistakes can delay the process or even lead to a denial. Once submitted, it's a waiting game, but patience is key. Think of it as waiting for a rare plant to bloom—frustrating, but ultimately worth it.

Ignoring these legalities can lead to significant consequences. Non-compliance isn't just a minor infraction; it can cause substantial fines, or in extreme cases, legal action. Imagine explaining to a judge why you thought a backyard full of bobcats was a good idea. Beyond fines, there's also the heart-wrenching risk of confiscation. Authorities can swoop in and take your beloved pet away if you're found in violation of the law, leaving you with an empty enclosure and an even emptier heart. It's like losing a game of Monopoly because you forgot to collect $200 when passing "Go" only ten times worse.

So, where do you go for guidance if you're feeling lost? Local wildlife agencies are your best bet for up-to-date and reliable information. They can provide insights into specific requirements and help clarify any confusion. Exotic pet associations often offer legal advice and resources tailored to pet owners. These organizations can be like having a seasoned guide on a tricky hiking trail, leading you safely to your destination. Now that you're armed with this knowledge, you can approach exotic pet ownership with confidence and peace of mind, knowing you're on the right side of the law.

Understanding the Exotic Pet Trade: Ethical Sourcing

Imagine the exotic pet trade as a bustling global marketplace where every stall holds a creature more fascinating than the last. While this trade can introduce you to delightful companions, it also comes with a hefty dose of ethical dilemmas. The choice between wild-caught and captive-bred animals is at the heart of these issues. Wild-caught animals, often taken from their natural habitats, face the stress of captivity and transportation, not to mention the ecological impact of removing them from their ecosystems. Captive-bred animals are born and raised in controlled environments, typically resulting in healthier pets with fewer behavioral issues. Opting for captive-bred pets helps reduce the demand for wild captures, preserving delicate ecosystems and minimizing the stress these animals endure.

The black market trade is another shadowy aspect of this industry. A rogue operation, often disguised as legitimate business, traffics endangered species under the radar. This illegal trade not only threatens the survival of certain species but also undermines conservation efforts. By choosing pets sourced from ethical and legal channels, you're standing against this damaging trade. You're not just a pet owner; you're a conservation ally, playing a part in the survival of species teetering on the brink of extinction. Supporting reputable breeders and sellers ensures that your purchase doesn't inadvertently fund these black-market activities, keeping your conscience as clear as your pet's terrarium glass.

So, how do you spot an ethical source in this vast market? Begin by searching for breeders and sellers with the credentials. Certification and accreditation from recognized animal welfare organizations are good indicators of ethical practices. These credentials show the breeders adhere to high standards of animal care and welfare. Transparency is another hallmark of a reputable source. Ethical breeders openly share information about their breeding practices, the origins of their animals, and their health records. This openness ensures you're not left in the dark about your pet's past and promotes trust between you and the seller. It's like buying a car with a full service history—you know exactly what you're getting into.

Conservation plays a pivotal role in ethical sourcing. Supporting breeders who contribute to conservation efforts is not only responsible, but also rewarding. These breeders often engage in projects that aim to protect natural habitats and enhance species survival. By choosing species with sustainable populations, you're ensuring that your pet doesn't contribute to the decline of wild populations. Some breeders even donate a portion of their proceeds to conservation projects, thus enabling you to directly support the protection of endangered species. It's like getting a pet and a ticket to help save the world in one go.

Captive breeding programs are the unsung heroes of the conservation world. These programs help reduce pressure on wild populations by providing a steady supply of animals bred in captivity. They also enhance genetic diversity, which is crucial for species survival. A well-managed captive breeding program can act as a genetic reservoir, safeguarding species from extinction. By opting for pets from these programs, you're not just gaining a new family member; you're supporting efforts to preserve biodiversity. It's a win-win scenario where you get a healthy pet, and the species gets a fighting chance.

The exotic pet trade is a complex and multifaceted world. While it offers opportunities for unique companionship, it also calls for responsible and ethical decision-making. By understanding the implications of your choices and supporting ethical practices, you can enjoy the thrill of exotic pet ownership while contributing positively to the greater good.

Conservation and Impact: The Broader Implications of Ownership

Imagine your exotic pet as a tiny ambassador for its species, representing the delicate balance of biodiversity and ecosystem health. When you welcome an exotic pet into your home, you're not just gaining a new companion; you're also contributing to a broader ecological narrative. Understanding the conservation status of various exotic species is crucial. Habitat destruction and other human activities threaten and endanger some exotic pets, pushing them to the brink of extinction. The availability of these species in the pet trade can often reflect their status in the wild. Habitat destruction is a major driver behind the scarcity of these creatures—think of it as Mother Nature's eviction notice, where deforestation and urban sprawl push animals from their homes. By being aware of these factors, you can make informed decisions that align with conservation goals, ensuring your pet ownership doesn't contribute to biodiversity loss.

Owning an exotic pet can have unexpected ecological implications, much like the ripple effects of a stone thrown into a pond. Introducing non-native species into local ecosystems poses significant risks, as these animals can become invasive if accidentally released. Invasive species are the uninvited guests at a party, often out-competing native wildlife for resources and disrupting ecological balance. They can wreak havoc on local flora and fauna, sometimes leading to the decline or extinction of indigenous species. Preventing accidental releases is crucial; it's like keeping the lid tightly sealed on a jar of pickles—you don't want those tangy critters spilling out and causing chaos. Secure enclosures and responsible handling practices are key strategies to avoid such mishaps, ensuring your pet remains an enriching part of your life without becoming an ecological villain.

When selecting an exotic pet, consider the ecological footprint of your choice. Some species have minimal environmental impact because of sustainable populations and well-managed breeding programs. By choosing pets from these backgrounds, you're minimizing your footprint and supporting responsible pet ownership. Think of it as choosing a hybrid car over a gas-guzzler—every little help. Your pet ownership can support conservation initiatives. Many breeders and organizations channel funds into conservation projects, using protects natural habitats and endangered species. By purchasing from these sources, you're indirectly supporting efforts to conserve and restore ecosystems. It's like getting a two-for-one deal, where you gain a beloved pet and contribute to global conservation efforts.

There are inspiring examples of conservation programs that have successfully integrated exotic pets into broader ecological goals. Breeding programs have bolstered wild populations, serving as genetic reservoirs that safeguard species from extinction. These programs are the superheroes of conservation, stepping in when wild populations dwindle and ensuring a future for endangered species. Educational outreach programs also play a vital role in promoting species preservation. By raising awareness and fostering appreciation for exotic animals, these initiatives encourage responsible ownership and conservation-minded decisions. They transform curiosity into a catalyst for change, inspiring individuals to act to support wildlife and habitats. Your role as an exotic pet owner can extend beyond the walls of your home, contributing to these positive conservation efforts and making a meaningful impact on the world around you.

Legal Responsibilities: Compliance and Documentation

Owning an exotic pet is like having a quirky, lovable roommate who occasionally throws wild, yet endearing, parties. To maintain peace, it's crucial to stay up-to-date with the ever-changing list of laws and regulations governing your pet's presence. These rules can shift like dunes in a desert windstorm, so it's essential to renew any permits and licenses on time. Missing a renewal deadline can lead to unnecessary headaches, much like forgetting your anniversary. Staying informed about new legislation is equally important. Laws change slower than chameleons and blend into their surroundings; what was acceptable yesterday might be prohibited tomorrow. Monitoring updates ensures you avoid any unpleasant surprises, like unannounced visits from local authorities.

Documentation is another key piece of this legal puzzle. Think of it as your pet's paper trail, proving that everything is open. Having solid records of legal acquisition is crucial. This includes receipts, permits, and any other documentation that verifies your pet's journey from the breeder to your home. If you're involved in breeding or selling, meticulous record-keeping is non-negotiable. Document every transaction and interaction, as these records can serve as evidence in the event of any disputes that may arise. It's like having a well-organized photo album—each page tells a part of the story, and together they provide a comprehensive picture of your pet's life.

Even with all the correct documents in hand, disputes can arise, much like unexpected rain on a sunny day. Navigating these situations requires a mix of diplomacy and legal savvy. Mediation provides a peaceful path to resolution, enabling all parties to discuss their concerns in a controlled and structured environment. If things escalate beyond a dragon's breath, legal representation may be necessary. Having a lawyer who understands exotic pet laws can be invaluable, offering guidance and advocacy when you need it most. Accessing resources for legal support can make a world of difference, providing you with the tools and knowledge to address conflicts effectively. It's like having an umbrella in a storm—protection when you need it, ensuring you stay dry and unflustered.

Staying informed about the law is the best way to avoid problems. Staying informed about your responsibilities and any changes in the law is like having a map in uncharted territory. Taking part in workshops and seminars can be enlightening, offering insights and updates that keep you ahead of the curve. You'll learn a lot about legal rules at these events; they'll give you the latest information and best practices. Joining exotic pet advocacy groups can also be beneficial. These communities provide not just updates but also support and camaraderie, connecting you with fellow pet owners who share your passion. It's a bit like joining a club where everyone speaks the same language, offering advice and encouragement as you navigate the legal landscape.

Interactive Element: Legal Checklist for Exotic Pet Owners

- Keep your legal responsibilities in check with this handy

checklist:

- Have you renewed your permits and licenses on time?

- Are you up-to-date with the latest laws and regulations affecting your pet?

- Do you have all the documentation for your pet's acquisition and any breeding or sales activities?

- Are you prepared for potential legal disputes with access to mediation or legal representation?

- Have you taken part in workshops and joined advocacy groups to stay informed?

Maintaining compliance and thorough documentation is not just about avoiding trouble; it's about ensuring a safe environment for both you and your pet. It's like being the best host in a neighborhood where everyone's watching—staying on top of your game keeps everything running smoothly.

Ethical Dilemmas: Making Informed Choices

Owning an exotic pet is like hosting a unique guest in your home—it's exciting but comes with a fair share of ethical considerations. As you navigate the thrilling world of exotic pet ownership, you'll encounter dilemmas that require balancing personal desires with ecological responsibility. You might yearn for a vibrant macaw or a sleek python. However, these creatures come with their own set of needs that can be as high maintenance as a rock star's tour demands. It's essential to assess whether you can provide an environment that meets not just the basic needs of these pets, but also their emotional and social requirements. Many species require extensive care and attention, and it's crucial to weigh your capability to meet these demands without causing undue stress or harm to the animal. It's like wanting to adopt a Great Dane when you live in a studio apartment—you need to consider if your lifestyle can accommodate such a commitment.

When pondering your next exotic pet, take a moment to reflect on the broader implications of your decision. This isn't just about the immediate joy of having a unique companion. It involves a long-term commitment to their care, which can span decades. Consider the welfare implications of exotic pet breeding. Some species suffer in captivity, and supporting breeders who prioritize profit over welfare perpetuates a cycle of suffering. It's like buying a piece of fast fashion that falls apart after a few wears—cheap in the short term but costly for the environment. Think critically about the origins of your pet and the impact of your choices. Are you inadvertently supporting practices that harm the very creatures you admire? By engaging in ethical decision-making, you ensure that your pet's well-being is at the forefront of your choices.

To make informed and ethical choices, adopt a decision-making framework, much like a blueprint guiding your actions. Consider using ethical decision-making models that help evaluate the potential consequences of pet ownership. These frameworks encourage you to weigh the pros and cons of your choices, just like you'd consider the nutritional info on a candy bar before indulging. Engage with ethical discussions in pet communities, both online and in-person. These forums can be invaluable in offering diverse perspectives and experiences, helping you navigate the murky waters of ethical pet ownership. They're like a book club, but instead of discussing the latest thriller, you're debating the merits of different breeding practices.

Stories of ethical challenges and resolutions can provide valuable insights into the complexities of exotic pet ownership. Take, for example, the case of a family that adopted a beautiful but demanding parrot. They soon realized they couldn't meet its needs, leading to a hard decision to re-home the bird. This experience taught them the importance of considering the long-term implications of their choices. Similarly, there are stories of owners who have become advocates for ethical pet trade practices, supporting the rights of these animals and promoting responsible ownership. These narratives powerfully remind us that moral dilemmas are an integral part of the journey, and that no one decides in isolation. By learning from these stories, you equip yourself with the knowledge and empathy needed to make informed and compassionate choices.

Advocacy and Awareness: Becoming a Responsible Owner

Owning an exotic pet is just the beginning; being an advocate for their well-being is where the adventure truly takes off. Imagine for a moment that your pet, whether it's a colorful parrot or a slinky snake, could speak for the wild companions it left behind. As a responsible owner, you have the power to amplify that voice. One way to achieve this is by participating in awareness campaigns and events that promote responsible pet ownership and conservation. These gatherings are like pep rallies, where passionate individuals come together to support the cause of exotic pets. By joining in, you not only gain valuable insights, but also contribute to a collective effort that promotes better standards and practices within the exotic pet community.

But advocacy doesn't stop at participating in events; it extends to collaborating with wildlife conservation organizations. These groups work tirelessly to protect natural habitats and the creatures that inhabit them. By partnering with them, you can help support their initiatives, from habitat restoration projects to educational programs that teach communities about the importance of biodiversity. Imagine being part of a team that plants trees to restore a parrot's natural habitat or works on a campaign to save a species from extinction. Your involvement can make a tangible difference, ensuring that future generations can enjoy the wonder of exotic animals both in the wild and as part of our lives.

Education plays a crucial role in promoting ethical ownership. Sharing your experiences and knowledge with others can ignite a spark of curiosity and responsibility to potential pet owners. Consider hosting workshops or seminars on exotic pet care. These events can be enlightening, offering practical tips and fostering discussions about the challenges and joys of owning exotic pets. You could also write articles or start a blog dedicated to responsible ownership. By doing so, you create a platform where your insights and experiences can reach a wider audience, influencing others to make informed and ethical decisions.

Building a supportive community is vital for both personal growth and the broader cause. Connect with like-minded individuals by joining local and online exotic pet clubs. These groups serve as hubs for sharing experiences, advice, and support. Networking with conservationists and pet enthusiasts can open doors to new opportunities and collaborations. It's like joining a club where everyone shares your passion and is eager to help you succeed. Together, you can brainstorm solutions to everyday challenges, share success stories, and celebrate the joys of owning exotic pets.

Success stories abound in the world of exotic pet advocacy. Community-led efforts have successfully changed local regulations, improving conditions for both pets and their owners. These initiatives show the power of collective action and its positive impact on pet welfare standards. For example, some communities have rallied to establish new guidelines for the care and housing of exotic pets, ensuring they receive the proper attention and the environment they deserve. These changes not only benefit the pets, but also foster a sense of pride and responsibility within the community.

As we conclude this chapter, remember that advocating for the welfare of exotic pets is a journey with no final destination. Every action you take, no matter how small, contributes to a more significant movement that seeks to improve the lives of these fascinating creatures. Whether you're taking part in events, sharing knowledge, or building a community, your efforts matter. Together, we can build a world where exotic pets are cherished companions and ambassadors for their wild counterparts. With this foundation in place, we're ready to explore the next exciting chapter in our exploration of exotic pet care.

Chapter 7: Building a Supportive Community

You're Not Alone—Thriving Together Through Connection

I magine you're at home, sipping your morning coffee, when suddenly your bearded dragon does the cha-cha across its terrarium. You think, "Is this normal?" In these moments, having a supportive community of fellow exotic pet owners is like having a lifeline. Welcome to the world of online forums and social media groups, where enthusiasts gather to share stories, swap tips, and occasionally debate whether crickets or mealworms reign supreme. Navigating these digital spaces can seem daunting at first, but they're teeming with passionate folks eager to help you and your scaly, furry, or feathered friend thrive.

To get started, finding the right online community is crucial. Think of it like choosing a new favorite coffee shop; you want a place that feels welcoming and offers what you need. Websites like Our Reptile Forum offer reptile owners a place to find information and connect with others. They have care guides and discussions about many reptiles. This forum offers a treasure trove of information with specific sub-forums for various species, allowing you to dive deep into the care and behavior of your particular pet. It's like having a library, but with actual people who can answer your questions in real time. Social media, too, has a plethora of groups dedicated to exotic pets. These groups, often found on Facebook or Reddit, are great for sharing experiences and advice. They're like a virtual roundtable where everyone brings their own quirky pet tales.

The benefits of these online communities are as bountiful as a buffet at a seafood restaurant. They provide real-time feedback, allowing you to ask questions and get answers faster than you can say "tortoise." Many seasoned pet owners frequent these forums, eager to pass on their knowledge like wise old wizards. These platforms also offer camaraderie, connecting you with people who understand the unique joys and challenges of exotic pet ownership. It's reassuring to know you're not alone in wondering why your snake prefers to nap in its water bowl. Online communities can also be a source of comfort, especially when you're faced with challenging situations. Whether it's a medical concern or a quirky behavior that has you puzzled, these groups can provide insights and support.

When engaging in these online discussions, the key is to contribute positively and benefit from the shared knowledge. Share your experiences and insights without hesitation; your story might be exactly what another pet owner needs to hear. Respectful communication is essential, especially when opinions differ. Remember, it's not about winning an argument over whether leopard geckos are better than crested geckos—it's about learning and sharing. Conflict resolution skills come in handy when navigating disagreements. Approach discussions with an open mind, and you'll find that even the most heated debates can lead to new insights.

Of course, not every piece of advice found online is golden. Misinformation and biased claims can lurk, much like that last stubborn cricket hiding in your gecko's tank. To discern reliable advice from the not-so-great, always check the credibility of information sources. Look for consistency in the advice given and verify it against reputable sources. Recognize biased or unverified claims by seeking evidence or testimonials from multiple users. It's like being a detective, piecing together clues to find the truth. If a recommendation seems too good to be true, it probably is. Always approach advice with a healthy dose of skepticism and curiosity.

Interactive Element: Online Community Checklist

Before diving into the online world of exotic pet communities, consider:

- Platform Suitability: Does the forum or group focus on your pet's species?

- User Feedback: Are there experienced members offering

valuable insights?

- Community Rules: Is respectful communication encouraged?

- Source Verification: Can you verify the information with reputable sources?

- Personal Contribution: Are you ready to share your experiences and learn from others?

By following this checklist, you'll find a supportive online community that enriches your exotic pet ownership experience.

Local Exotic Pet Groups: Meetups and Networking

Imagine stepping into a lively room buzzing with fellow reptile enthusiasts, each person more excited than the last to chat about their beloved companions. Local exotic pet groups and meetups offer a unique opportunity to connect personally with others who share your interests. These gatherings often feature monthly meetings with guest speakers who dive into topics like uncommon health concerns or the latest in habitat technology. It's like attending a mini-conference tailored just for you and your scaly friend. Not only do you get to hear from experts, but you also gain hands-on experience through workshops dedicated to habitat building and care techniques. Picture yourself learning to construct the perfect vivarium, guided by someone who's done it a hundred times before. These experiences are not only educational but also empower you to provide the best care possible for your pet.

In-person networking at these meetups is invaluable. Face-to-face interactions offer something special that online interactions cannot replicate. When you meet someone who shares your passion, the bond is instant. You can swap stories about your pets' quirks, like how your gecko insists on sleeping upside down, and share resources like where to find the best deals on cricket food. You might even borrow a heat lamp or trading cuttings from a lush plant for your terrarium. These meetups foster long-lasting friendships with fellow enthusiasts who understand the joys and challenges of exotic pet ownership. You might find a mentor who guides you through your first hibernation period or a buddy to visit reptile expos with. It's a community where everyone supports each other, making the exotic pet world a little less intimidating and a lot more fun.

Finding and joining local groups might seem daunting, but it's easier than you think. Start by searching online directories and social platforms like Meetup.com, which often lists events and groups in your area. Pet shops can also be a goldmine of information; staff members are usually in the know about local gatherings and often have flyers or contacts for group organizers. Once you've found a group that piques your interest, dive in headfirst. Attend a meeting, introduce yourself, and don't hesitate to ask questions. These groups are typically welcoming, and they love seeing fresh faces. Being an active member means showing up, taking part, and offering your own insights when you can. Your experience, no matter how limited, is valuable and can contribute to the group's collective knowledge.

If you're feeling adventurous, consider organizing a community event yourself. Hosting a pet care workshop or seminar can be incredibly rewarding. Picture leading a session on the nutritional needs of iguanas, complete with a salad buffet for demonstration. Or organize a group visit to a local zoo or wildlife center, providing an opportunity for members to see exotic animals in a unique setting and perhaps gain inspiration for their habitats. These activities not only build community, but also spread knowledge and enthusiasm. They can be as straightforward or as elaborate as you like, from casual backyard meetups to more structured events with guest speakers and planned activities. The key is to bring people together, share knowledge, and celebrate the love for exotic pets.

Sharing Experiences: The Power of Storytelling

Picture this: you're sitting at your kitchen table, sipping a hot cup of tea, while your parrot, perched nearby, recounts its latest escapade to you. It mimics the doorbell, your laugh, and even the neighbor's dog—all with impeccable timing. This little feathered friend has a story to tell, and so do you. Sharing your pet ownership stories isn't just about entertainment; it's about fostering empathy, learning, and connection. When you open up about the challenges and successes you've faced, you provide others with a window into your world. These narratives serve as powerful tools for illustrating problem-solving techniques, like how you coaxed your shy snake out of hiding or finally got your tortoise to stop redecorating its enclosure. The more we share, the more we learn from each other, and the stronger our community becomes.

Crafting and sharing impactful stories is a bit like baking a cake—you need the right ingredients and a good recipe. Start with a clear beginning, middle, and end. Set the scene by introducing your pet and the particular challenge or triumph you're focusing on. Engage your audience with relatable struggles, like the time your iguana decided it was the perfect moment to take a nap in your laundry basket. Highlight the steps you took to overcome these hurdles, emphasizing any creative solutions you discovered along the way. Wrap up with the outcome, whether it's a newfound solution or a humorous realization that sometimes, pets will be pets. By structuring your stories thoughtfully, you can inspire and educate others, turning your personal experiences into valuable lessons.

Now that your story is ready to share, where do you spread the word? Many platforms offer the perfect stage for your tales. Blogging or vlogging about your pet experiences can reach a wide audience, allowing you to connect with fellow enthusiasts worldwide. These digital diaries can become a treasure trove of insights, providing both amusement and education. If the written word is more your style, consider contributing to newsletters or community publications. These outlets provide a more intimate setting for sharing your stories, reaching readers who are keen to learn from your experiences. Whether you prefer the visual flair of a vlog or the thoughtful prose of a blog post, these platforms allow you to share your passion with a community that appreciates every feathered, scaled, and furry detail.

The impact of storytelling on the community can be profound. When individuals share their experiences, they create ripples of influence that can lead to real change. Take, for example, a story about a pet owner who discovered a new way to enrich their lizard's habitat, sparking a community initiative to create a shared resource library for habitat ideas. Another tale might focus on a breakthrough in training, leading to improved pet care practices across the community. These narratives inspire others to try alternative approaches, fostering a spirit of innovation and collaboration. Through storytelling, we not only celebrate our pets, but also contribute to a collective pool of knowledge that benefits everyone involved.

Textual Element: Reflection Section

Consider when your pet taught you something valuable, whether it was a lesson in patience, creativity, or simply the joy of living in the moment. Write your story, focusing on the emotions and insights you gained. Think about how sharing this experience could inspire others.

In the end, storytelling isn't just about recounting events. It's about connecting, learning, and growing together. Each story we share adds a new thread to the rich tapestry of our community, weaving together a network of support and understanding that strengthens with every tale told. So, grab that metaphorical pen and start sharing your adventures. Your story could be the one that makes a difference.

Continuous Learning: Workshops and Seminars

Owning an exotic pet is a bit like being in a never-ending science class where the lessons are as fascinating as they are unpredictable. Perhaps your iguana has developed an unexpected fondness for your favorite houseplant, or your snake is giving you a series of looks that hold meaning. Enter workshops and seminars, your best allies in the quest for knowledge expansion and skill development. These events offer you the chance to learn new care techniques directly from seasoned experts, who may have the perfect solution to your pet's unique habits.

They also keep you updated on emerging research and trends, helping you stay at the cutting edge of exotic pet care. Think of seminars as your educational pit stops, where you refuel with fresh insights and practical tips that you can apply in your daily life.

Finding relevant educational events might seem like searching for a needle in a haystack, but fear not! Many organizations dedicate themselves to the welfare of exotic pets and regularly host workshops and seminars. Following these organizations on social media or subscribing to their newsletters can help keep you informed about upcoming events. You may also find event bulletins at local pet shops or veterinary clinics, which often have connections to the broader pet community. Websites dedicated to exotic pet care frequently list events and gatherings, providing you with a roadmap to the best learning opportunities in your area. The key is to stay engaged and curious, always on the lookout for new chances to expand your understanding.

When you attend these educational events, active participation is the key benefit that makes the experience truly enriching. Before you go, prepare a list of questions you want to ask the experts, focusing on areas where you seek clarity or new insights. This approach ensures that you leave the event with actionable information tailored to your needs. During the seminar, don't shy away from networking with other attendees. These connections can lead to shared insights and might just introduce you to new friends who completely understand your pet's quirky behaviors. Engaging with others not only enhances your learning experience but also broadens your support network, providing you with a community of like-minded individuals who share your passion.

Consider the impact that certain workshops and seminars have had on participants. Imagine a hands-on training session in advanced habitat management, where attendees get to roll up their sleeves and learn how to create the perfect environment for their pets. Participants leave with newfound confidence, armed with practical skills they can implement immediately. Or picture a seminar focused on ethical breeding practices and conservation, where experts share their knowledge on how to ensure that your pet's lineage supports broader conservation efforts. These events not only educate but also inspire, empowering you to make informed decisions that benefit both your pet and the exotic pet community at large.

Building a Support Network: Friends, Family, and Experts

Imagine for a moment that you're the proud owner of a charismatic chameleon. Its rapid color changes never cannot amaze you, but suddenly, it seems a little off. Perhaps it's not as vibrant as before, or maybe it's spending too much time in its hide. When faced with such moments, having a robust support network is invaluable. This network can be a blend of friends, family, and experts, each offering their own unique support. Friends and family provide the emotional backing you need. They're the ones who listen to your tales of chameleon adventures, even if they don't always understand why you're so excited about the latest molt. Their encouragement is like a warm cup of tea on a chilly day, offering comfort and reassurance. Involving them in pet care routines can be a delightful bonding experience. Invite them over to observe feeding time or share educational resources that explain why your reptile needs a heat lamp. By engaging them, you not only educate but also create a shared experience, turning solitary care tasks into opportunities for connection. One delightful example involves a family who turned their living room into a mini-reptile sanctuary. Each member took on a role, from handling the feeding to maintaining the humidity levels. This not only strengthened their bond but also ensured that their pet received the best care possible.

Experts, on the other hand, provide the professional advice and guidance that friends and family might lack. Veterinarians are the go-to for medical advice, helping you navigate everything from dietary needs to mysterious symptoms. Reaching out to behaviorists can be incredibly beneficial if your pet's actions are perplexing or if you need help with training. These professionals are like the lifeguards of the exotic pet world, ready to dive in when the waters get choppy. Their expertise can turn confusion into clarity, offering solutions and peace of mind. Consider the story of a pet owner whose iguana developed a persistent health problem. After consulting with a knowledgeable vet, they could adjust the iguana's diet and habitat, leading to a remarkable improvement in its health. This expert intervention not only eased stress but also enhanced the quality of life for both the pet and the owner.

Building a support network is like crafting a safety net, ensuring that someone's always there to catch you when things get tricky. It's a diverse mix of resources, each playing a vital role. By involving friends and family, you gain emotional support and shared experiences. Experts offer the guidance and knowledge necessary to tackle more complex issues. This comprehensive network is a testament to the idea that no pet owner is an island. You don't have to face challenges alone;

there are people and professionals eager to help you and your exotic companion thrive. Sharing the journey with others transforms pet ownership from a solitary endeavor into a collaborative and enriching experience, filled with opportunities for learning and growth.

Troubleshooting Isolation: Overcoming Support Gaps

Having an exotic pet can sometimes feel you're on a deserted island. It's just you, your gecko, and a lot of crickets. The unique needs and behaviors of exotic pets can lead to feelings of loneliness or overwhelm, especially when local resources are as rare as a two-headed snake. Many pet owners find themselves in a bind, with few nearby communities to turn to for advice or camaraderie. The absence of local resources can make finding relatable experiences a challenge, leaving you feeling like the only iguana enthusiast in town. It's not uncommon to feel a bit isolated when everyone else seems to have dogs and cats, animals that come with entire aisles dedicated to them at the pet store.

So, what's a reptile-loving human to do? Fear not! There are solutions to bridge these support gaps and connect with fellow exotic pet enthusiasts. Begin by searching for online communities that cater to your pet's specific needs. These digital havens offer a wealth of knowledge and experiences from people who are just as passionate about their scaly or feathered friends as you are. While I covered online options earlier, don't overlook the value of building relationships with local pet stores or veterinarians. These experts can offer valuable insights, recommend relevant resources, and even introduce you to other local owners. Many pet store staff members are enthusiasts themselves and might connect with local meetups or fellow customers who share your interests.

Taking initiative is key to overcoming isolation. Embrace your inner social butterfly (or should I say social gecko?) and start conversations with potential mentors or fellow pet owners. Volunteering at animal shelters can also be a fantastic way to meet like-minded individuals. Not only do you get to engage with animals, but you also gain valuable experience and connections. Shelters often welcome volunteers and may have exotic pets in need of care, giving you the chance to expand your skills and network. Your passion for exotic pets can open doors to relationships and opportunities you never imagined. All it takes is a bit of courage and a willingness to put yourself out there.

Let's look at some inspiring examples of individuals who successfully filled their support gaps. Take the story of a dedicated reptile owner who created a local club, bringing together others who shared their love for these unique creatures. What started as a small gathering in a community center quickly grew into a thriving group, complete with monthly meetings and guest speakers. This club became a lifeline for its members, offering support, education, and friendship. Another tale involves an owner who formed online friendships through social media groups, which eventually blossomed into real-world connections. These friendships led to group outings and even annual retreats, where members could swap stories and tips in person. These stories show that building a supportive network is not only possible but immensely rewarding.

As you navigate the world of exotic pet ownership, remember that you're not alone. The connections you make can transform your experience, turning isolation into a vibrant community of fellow enthusiasts. Embrace the opportunity to learn from others, share your own experiences, and grow together. This chapter has highlighted the importance of building a supportive community, helping to ensure that you and your exotic pet thrive. With these connections in place, you'll be well-prepared for whatever challenges come your way. Now, as we turn the page, we'll explore how to create a rich and fulfilling environment for both you and your pet, ensuring a harmonious and joyful companionship.

Chapter 8:
Enhancing the
Pet Ownership
Experience

From Routine
to Reward—Finding
Meaning in Every
Moment

Have you ever stared at your pet's tank, wishing it could be more than just a glass box with a heat lamp? Perhaps imagining it as a lush jungle or a serene desert oasis, rather than a boring terrarium. Bioactive vivarium's offer a natural habitat for your pet, supported by tiny animals that help maintain the environment. It's like having a slice of the Amazon in your living room, minus the pesky mosquitoes and the existential question of how you ended up with a chameleon that judges your taste in wallpaper.

These bioactive setups are not just a pretty face; they're all about replicating natural environments and promoting your pet's instincts. Picture your reptile as the star of its own nature documentary, where the habitat encourages behaviors like burrowing, climbing, or even an impromptu game of hide-and-seek with its favorite plant. And the best part? These ecosystems essentially take care of themselves, thanks to a self-sustaining cycle that minimizes your maintenance work to occasional tweaks. Your cleanup crew—comprising springtails and isopods—works tirelessly to break down organic waste, turning it into nutrients that support plant growth and keep odors in check. It's like having tiny, invisible maids who never ask for a day off or a Christmas bonus.

So, how do you create this mini-Eden? Start by selecting compatible plants and microfauna. Choose flora that can withstand your pet's not-so-gentle touch and thrive in similar humidity and temperature ranges. Ferns, pothos, and ficus are popular choices. They not only look fantastic but also improve air quality and offer hiding spots. Your microfauna, those industrious springtails and isopods, should match the biome you're replicating. These little guys, the backbone of your ecosystem, ensure efficient waste recycling into plant food. Next, consider the substrate layers for drainage and plant growth. A drainage layer, such as clay balls or gravel, is crucial to prevent water-logging and root rot. Above this, layer a mix of organic soil suited to your pet's biome needs, incorporating materials like coco coir and peat moss to provide a stable base for plants and burrowing critters.

Once your bioactive vivarium is up and running, ongoing care is crucial to maintain balance. Monitor plant health by checking for signs of wilt or discoloration. These could indicate nutritional deficiencies or improper lighting. Adjusting humidity levels is another key task, ensuring they align with your pet's natural habitat. Use a hygrometer to track these levels, and make tweaks as necessary, either by misting the enclosure or improving ventilation. Regularly check the health and population of your microfauna, as they play a vital role in your ecosystem's stability. If you notice a decline, it might be time to restock or adjust to environmental conditions.

Beyond practicality, bioactive vivarium's offer aesthetic perks that elevate your home decor from mundane to magnificent. Incorporating decorative elements that mimic natural landscapes can create a visually stunning habitat that rivals any Pinterest board. Use driftwood, rocks, and moss to craft a scene that looks like a page from National Geographic. Thoughtful lighting choices can highlight these features, casting an ethereal glow that captivates both you and your guests. Whether it's a spotlight on your snake's favorite perch or a gentle wash of light over your chameleon's leafy retreat, lighting can transform your setup into a veritable work of art.

Interactive Element: Vivarium Planning Guide

Jot down your ideas for your dream bioactive vivarium:

- Choose Your Plants: List three plant species that thrive in your pet's habitat conditions.

- Select Your Microfauna: Decide on the cleanup crew—springtails, isopods, or both?

- Substrate Layers: Describe the layers you'll use for drainage and plant support.

- Decorative Features: Sketch or note any decorative elements you'd like to include.

- Lighting Considerations: Plan how you'll highlight your vivarium's best features.

This planning guide can help you design a living masterpiece that serves as both a functional habitat and a stunning display.

Cultural Significance: Understanding Your Pet's Origins

Imagine your exotic pet as more than just a living room companion. They have a rich history that spans centuries, often deeply ingrained in the cultural fabric of societies around the globe. Take reptiles, for instance. In many indigenous cultures, these creatures were symbols of transformation and resilience. The snake, shedding its skin, became a metaphor for renewal and rebirth. In some Native American traditions, the turtle was revered as a symbol of longevity and perseverance, carrying the world on its back in creation myths. Respecting these cultural narratives can deepen your appreciation for your pet, transforming it from a simple resident of its tank to a living connection to ancient stories and values.

People in various societies have long-esteemed birds for their symbolism and beauty. Artists often depict parrots, with their vibrant plumage and remarkable ability to mimic sounds, as messengers between the human and divine realms. Their presence in the home was a conduit for wisdom and protection. In Hindu mythology, for example, parrots are associated with the goddess Saraswati, symbolizing knowledge and eloquence. Across different cultures, birds have been both revered and feared, with owls symbolizing wisdom in some traditions and harbingers of misfortune in others. Understanding these symbolic roles can enrich your interactions with your feathered friend, adding layers of meaning to your daily routines.

Knowledge of your pet's cultural origins can influence how you care for it. By incorporating traditional practices into modern care, you cultivate a deeper bond with your pet. Consider naming your pet based on its cultural significance or introducing elements of its historical habitat into its environment. For instance, if you own a snake, learning about its role in ancient mythologies might inspire you to create a habitat that reflects its natural surroundings, fostering an environment where your pet feels secure and at home. Such thoughtful gestures can help bridge the past and present, making your pet care routine not just an act of maintenance but a celebration of history and heritage.

To delve into your pet's cultural history, start with anthropological studies and historical texts. You can find treasure troves of information in libraries and online databases; these sources reveal how different cultures view and interact with your pet's species. Connect with cultural experts or communities who can provide firsthand accounts and interpretations, enriching your understanding. Local museums or cultural centers may host exhibits or talks related to your pet's origins, giving further opportunities for exploration. These resources can illuminate the stories and traditions that surround your pet, sparking curiosity and enriching your experience of ownership.

Consider the story of a friend who discovered that her parrot was not just a chatty companion but also a link to her ancestral roots. Her research revealed how her ancestors' mythology revered parrots as embodiments of freedom and communication. This discovery transformed her relationship with her pet, infusing their interactions with a sense of continuity and respect. Similarly, another pet owner found a new appreciation for his tortoise upon learning about its symbolic role in ancient Chinese culture, where it was a symbol of wisdom and longevity. These stories show how understanding cultural backgrounds can enhance the pet ownership experience, turning simple interactions into meaningful exchanges.

With this newfound perspective, your pet becomes more than just an animal in your care. It becomes a living symbol of history and tradition, a reminder of the diverse ways humans have connected with the animal kingdom throughout the ages. This awareness adds depth to your role as a pet owner, encouraging a more mindful and respectful approach to care. As you explore your pet's cultural origins, you'll find that each discovery enriches your bond, transforming your home into a sanctuary of learning and appreciation.

Photography and Documentation: Capturing Your Journey

Think of your exotic pet as a tiny, yet captivating performer on the stage of your life. Capturing these moments through photography and journaling isn't just about snapping a cute picture or jotting down a few notes. It's about creating a tapestry of memories that chronicles your pet's milestones and growth. Imagine flipping through a visual diary years from now, where each photo and entry evokes the joy and challenges of your pet ownership adventure. From the first day you brought home that inquisitive little gecko to the triumphant moment your parrot finally learned to whistle your favorite tune, documenting these experiences allows you to track progress and reflect on the journey you've shared with your scaly or feathery friend.

To capture high-quality images of your exotic pet, consider the magic of natural light. It's like nature's very own Instagram filter, enhancing colors and details without a single app. Try photographing your pet during the soft, golden hours of early morning or late afternoon, when the light is gentle and flattering. If your pet is a bit of a live wire, darting around its enclosure faster than you can say "cheese," you might need to employ some nifty techniques for photographing moving subjects. A fast shutter speed can help freeze those action-packed moments, while a bit of patience and a steady hand can work wonders. Remember, the goal is to capture your pet's personality in all its quirky glory, whether they're striking a pose or caught mid-leap.

Sharing your pet photos and stories can foster a sense of community and connection with fellow pet enthusiasts. Consider building an online portfolio or blog where you can showcase your beloved creatures. This platform can serve as a creative outlet and a space to engage with others who share your passion. Social media pet communities are thriving hubs of inspiration and support. By sharing your own experiences, you contribute to a collective narrative that celebrates the joys and challenges of exotic pet ownership. It's like joining a global conversation, where each post and comment strengthens the bond between pet owners scattered across the world.

Organizing and preserving your documentation requires a bit of creativity and planning. Creating digital albums or scrapbooks can help you keep track of your pet's journey, allowing you to revisit cherished memories with a simple click or page flip. Consider printing and framing your favorite images to display them proudly in your home. These visual reminders can serve as conversation starters and daily affirmations of the special bond you share with your pet. Whether you opt for a minimalist photo book or a colorful collage of snapshots, the key is to create a system that reflects your personal style and keeps these memories easily accessible.

Textual Element: Pet Photography **Checklist**

Use this checklist to guide your next pet photoshoot:

- Choose Lighting: Opt for natural light during early morning or late afternoon.

- Camera Settings: Use a fast shutter speed for action shots.

- Capture Personality: Focus on showcasing your pet's unique traits.

- Organize Photos: Consider creating digital albums for easy access.

- Share Stories: Engage with online communities to connect with fellow pet lovers.

This checklist can help you capture the essence of your pet, creating a visual narrative that complements your shared experiences.

Mindful Pet Ownership: Balancing Responsibilities and Joy

Imagine your exotic pet as your little mindfulness guru, teaching you the art of being present with a wag of its tail or the flutter of its wings. Mindful pet ownership is about savoring every moment you spend with your pet, from cleaning their habitat to enjoying a quiet evening together. It's about practicing gratitude for the companionship they bring into your life, reminding you to pause and appreciate the simple joy of their presence. Whether it's that gentle rustling sound they make during feeding time or the way they tilt their head when they're curious about your antics, these moments are golden opportunities to be present and connected.

Balancing pet care responsibilities with your enjoyment doesn't have to feel like a juggling act. It's more like a dance, where you find the rhythm that suits both you and your pet. Scheduling time for both care tasks and leisure activities ensures neither aspect feels overwhelming. Perhaps you start your day with a feeding routine while sipping your morning coffee, turning a mundane task into a peaceful ritual. Or perhaps you find joy in the routine interactions, such as talking to your parrot while preparing dinner, turning it into a two-way conversation. The key is to weave these moments into your day so seamlessly that they feel like a natural extension of your life.

The emotional benefits of approaching pet care with mindfulness are profound. Focused, intentional care reduces stress, transforming what could be a chore into a moment of tranquility. This attentiveness deepens the bond between you and your pet, creating a relationship built on mutual presence and understanding. Your pet thrives on the attention and care, responding with their unique brand of affection, whether it's a gentle nuzzle or a playful chirp. It's a cycle of give and take, where the more present you are, the more rewarding the relationship becomes.

Incorporating mindful practices into pet care can be as simple as taking a few moments to breathe deeply and center yourself before interacting with your pet. Engage in meditation sessions where you sit quietly with your pet, observing their behaviors without judgment. This not only calms your mind but also allows you to connect with your pet on a deeper level. Journaling reflections on your daily interactions can also be a powerful tool, helping you document the brief moments that bring joy and insight. It's a way to capture the essence of your relationship with your pet, creating a written record of your shared journey.

One pet owner found that by spending a few minutes each evening reflecting on her interactions with her iguana, she became more attuned to its needs and moods. This simple act of mindfulness transformed her approach to care, fostering a deeper connection with her scaly companion. Another owner discovered that starting his day with a short meditation session alongside his snake helped him begin each morning with a sense of calm and focus. These practices, while simple, can have a profound impact on both you and your pet, enhancing the quality of your time together and enriching your overall experience.

Personal Growth Through Pet Ownership: Reflecting on Lessons Learned

Owning an exotic pet is like signing up for a crash course in patience and adaptability. You quickly discover that no two days are alike when you're living with a creature that might decide today's the day to re-decorate its terrarium by flinging substrate everywhere. As you learn to navigate the ups and downs of pet care, you also find yourself growing as a person. Patience becomes your ally when your chameleon refuses to eat anything but the most elusive crickets, and adaptability is key when your snake decides to shed its skin at midnight, prompting an unexpected late-night cleaning session. Through these challenges, you develop a deeper empathy and sense of responsibility, not just for your pet, but in other areas of your life as well.

Reflecting on these experiences can be enlightening. Consider keeping a journal where you jot down personal growth milestones and insights gained from your time with your pet. You might notice changes in your perspectives or habits that you hadn't expected. Perhaps you've become more observant, picking up on subtle cues from your pet that you apply to other aspects of life. Or maybe you've learned to appreciate the minor victories, like the first time your gecko successfully hunts its dinner, or your parrot mimics your laugh. These reflections not only help you track your progress, but also serve as reminders of the valuable lessons your pet has taught you.

Let me share a story of transformation. There was a man who, after adopting a stubborn iguana, found himself on a path of self-discovery. Initially frustrated by the iguana's selective eating habits and the peculiar need for precise humidity levels, he learned to adapt and found a purpose in meeting these challenges. This experience taught him patience, which he later applied to his work as a teacher, helping him connect with his students on a deeper level. Another individual, initially hesitant about taking on the responsibility of a pet, found a newfound sense of achievement in caring for a delicate tree frog. Each success, from maintaining the perfect balance in the frog's habitat to witnessing its first successful shed, filled her with a sense of accomplishment and confidence she hadn't felt before.

If you're looking to facilitate your own reflection and growth, consider engaging in activities and discussions that promote personal development. Workshops on personal growth and animal care can provide fresh perspectives and practical advice. Engaging with fellow pet owners in discussions, whether online or in person, can offer support and inspiration. These interactions can open your eyes to unique experiences and solutions, offering a sense of community and shared learning. They also remind you that you're not alone in facing the quirks and challenges of exotic pet ownership.

You might even find that the skills and insights you've gained translate into other areas of your life. Perhaps you've become more organized, thanks to the meticulous care routine your pet requires, or maybe you've developed a new appreciation for the natural world and its many wonders. By embracing these changes, you not only enhance your pet ownership experience but also enrich your own personal journey.

Embracing the Adventure: Celebrating Unique Companionship

Owning an exotic pet is like stepping into a world where every day brings a fresh surprise. Whether it's your gecko's unexpected nod of approval or your parrot's uncanny ability to mimic your morning grumble, these creatures offer companionship, unlike any other. Their individuality shines through the way they interact with their environment and with you. It's not just about feeding and cleaning; it's about witnessing the diverse behaviors and personalities each of these fascinating animals brings to the table. You might find your snake to be a quiet observer, while your bird actively seeks interaction, chirping along to your favorite tunes. Appreciating these unique traits can make pet ownership a continually rewarding experience.

As you journey with your exotic pet, you'll notice milestones and achievements that are worth celebrating. The first time your chameleon successfully catches its dinner with a lightning-fast flick of the tongue, or the moment your hedgehog trusts you enough to unfurl from its protective ball, these are victories worth noting. They offer a sense of progress and connection, reminding you of the shared experiences that deepen your bond. Mark these occasions with a small celebration, perhaps a new toy or an extra treat, to reinforce the positive growth you both experience.

Owning an exotic pet invites you to embrace a spirit of exploration and curiosity. Much like a detective following a trail of clues, you'll try out recent activities or environments to see what excites your pet. Maybe it's a jungle-themed terrarium setup for your frog, or a new climbing structure for your lizard to conquer. Exploring different enrichment opportunities keeps the experience fresh and engaging for both you and your pet. Consider introducing your pet to a new environment, like a safe outdoor space, where they can experience different textures and smells under your watchful eye. These adventures, big or small, foster a deeper connection and enhance your pet's quality of life.

Some of the most extraordinary pet-owner relationships are built on shared experiences and mutual understanding. There's the story of a woman whose tortoise became her gardening buddy, slowly but surely helping her prune her plants by munching on the lower leaves. Or the man whose parrot learned to mimic the sound of his car keys, making him chuckle every time he prepared to leave the house. These unique friendships highlight the depth and richness of the bonds you can form with your exotic pets. They remind us that companionship comes in many forms, and sometimes the quietest moments hold the most meaning.

To maximize the joy of pet ownership, consider setting goals and celebrating successes together. Whether it's training your pet to respond to a cue or overcoming a particular behavioral challenge, these milestones deserve acknowledgment. Creating traditions and rituals with your pet, such as a weekly enrichment day or a special treat on adoption anniversaries, can add layers of enjoyment to your relationship. These practices not only enhance your connection but also provide a framework for continued growth and discovery. By integrating these elements into your routine, you ensure that pet ownership remains a dynamic and rewarding adventure.

As our exploration of exotic pet ownership draws to an end, we've seen how these unique companions can transform our lives with their distinctive personalities and behaviors. By embracing the adventure, we open ourselves to new experiences and deepen our bonds. Whether celebrating milestones or exploring new enrichment opportunities, each moment spent with our pets enriches our lives and theirs. As we look forward to the next chapter, we'll delve into the practical aspects of pet care, ensuring that we continue to nurture these remarkable relationships with knowledge and responsibility.

Conclusion

C ongratulations! You've made it to the end of this wild ride through the world of exotic pets. Much like that iguana you've been eyeing, you've shown tenacity and curiosity, and that deserves a round of applause. Let's take a moment to reflect on the journey you've embarked upon.

Throughout this book, we've explored everything from the initial thrill of choosing your exotic companion to setting up their dream habitat. Remember that initial chapter where we talked about the motivation for owning an exotic pet? We discovered that these unique creatures aren't just for show; they're about building a meaningful connection. You've navigated the exciting yet ethical maze of the exotic pet marketplace and figured out which pet fits your lifestyle like a glove, or perhaps like a snake fits in its cozy hide.

We delved into the details of habitat setups, where you learned how to transform a basic enclosure into a luxurious, bioactive paradise. You even became a climate control expert, ensuring your pet feels right at home with perfect lighting, temperature, and humidity. Then there were those delectable discussions about dietary needs. I bet you could now craft a gourmet meal plan for your pet worthy of a Michelin star, ensuring they get all the nutrients they need without a side of avocado (because we all remember the "no avocados for reptiles" rule, right?).

Health and wellness took center stage as you learned to recognize signs of illness, schedule regular vet checkups, and even handle emergencies like a pro. You've become adept at socialization, handling, and understanding your pet's quirks, turning what might have been daily dilemmas into delightful interactions. Your exotic pet is now not just a pet but a cherished companion.

The important points from our time together? Exotic pet ownership is about responsibility, commitment, and a dash of adventure. You've learned the importance of ethical sourcing, legal compliance, and the impact of your choices on broader conservation efforts. But more than that, you've gained the skills to ensure your exotic pet thrives, from maintaining a clean habitat to engaging them with enrichment activities.

Now, here's your call to action:

Go forth and apply what you've learned. Whether you're a seasoned reptile wrangler or just starting your journey with a feisty parrot, use this knowledge to create a fulfilling life for you and your exotic buddy. Share your experiences, join communities, and continue learning. The world of exotic pets is vast, and there's always more to explore.

I would like to express my heartfelt gratitude for your interest in this book. Your dedication to providing the best care for your exotic pet is commendable. Thank you for allowing me to be part of your journey. You've shown that with the right tools and mindset, anyone can become a responsible and informed exotic pet owner.

I also invite you to stay engaged beyond these pages. Join online forums, attend local meetups, and take part in workshops. Keep the conversation going, share your stories, and inspire others. Your experiences and insights are invaluable to the exotic pet community.

Let's end on an inspirational note: Exotic pet ownership is not just a hobby; it's a journey of discovery, compassion, and joy. Each day with your pet is an opportunity to learn and grow. As you continue this adventure, remember that the bond you build with your exotic pet is unique and rewarding. Embrace the quirks, celebrate the milestones, and cherish every moment. Here's to a life filled with happy companionship and countless adventures with your exotic friend.

References

Exotic Animal Breeding: Responsible Practices vs. ... https://www.absoluteexoticssa.co.za/animal-blog-news/general-exotic-animal-articles-exotic-pet-content/315-exotic-animal-breeding-responsible-practices-vs-unethical-profit-driven-approaches

Exotic Pet Laws | Animal Legal & Historical Center https://www.animallaw.info/intro/exotic-pet-laws#:~:text=Some%20states%20and%20cities%20have,decide%20to%20limit%20exotic%20pets.

5 Best Exotic Pets for Beginners https://welovepets.care/pet-tips/5-best-exotic-pets-for-beginners%EF%BF%BC/

Exotic Pet Behavior: Understanding Their NaturalInstincts https://www.allcrittersvet.com/blog/exotic-pet-behavior-understanding-their-natural-instincts/

How to set up a bioactive terrarium https://exo-terra.com/explore/academy/bioactive/how-to-set-up-a-bioactive-terrarium/

Bioactive Enclosures - Creating a Tiny Ecosystem https://www.pri-web.org/blog-post/bioactive-enclosures

Temperature and Humidity Monitoring for Pet Reptiles ... https://www.sensorpush.com/articles/temperature-and-humidity-monitoring-for-pet-reptiles-and-amphibians?srsltid=AfmBOoqDq8mSjzS_SjLC4j5JnEYinDXfszZDE-Up9zml66t6Y27nu_one

Which Type of UVB Lamp Should I Use For My Reptile? https://www.reptilecentre.com/blogs/reptile-blog/which-type-of-uvb-lamp-should-i-use-for-my-reptile

Bon appétit! Nutritional Considerations for Exotic Pets https://www.isvma.org/wp-content/uploads/2022/10/BonAppetitNutritionalConsiderationsforExoticPets.pdf

Vitamins, Minerals, and Captive Herps https://www.lllreptile.com/articles/111-vitamins-minerals-and-captive-herps/?srsltid=AfmBOoqUwKmbcpBylvZzUTDjxlZZQufHXzUj8xXB6SegfAQf7Q7ukoJo

Iguanas: Feeding https://vcahospitals.com/know-your-pet/iguanas-feeding

Automated Cricket Feeder - Do you need one? https://www.chameleonforums.com/threads/automated-cricket-feeder-do-you-need-one.167774/

Recognizing Illness in Exotic Pets: Key Signs to WatchFor https://www.dovelewis.org/blog/recognizing-illness-exotic-pets-key-signs-watch

Vaccination Schedules for Exotic Pets https://www.mybeevet.com/blog/vaccination-schedules-for-exotic-pets/

How to Find an Exotic Vet https://oxbowanimalhealth.com/blog/how-to-find-an-exotic-vet/

Exotic Pet Emergency Care Guidelines https://www.iahvet.com.au/exotic-pet-emergency-care-guidelines/

10 Tips for Good Exotic Pet Care https://animalfamilyveterinarycare.com/blog/exotic-pet-care-davenport/

Exotic Pet Training and Socialization: Tips for Buildinga ... https://www.animalcareunlimited.com/blog/exotic-pet-training-and-socialization-tips-for-building-a-strong-bond-with-your-bird-reptile-or-small-mammal/

Overcoming Animal Phobias https://martinantony.com/wp-content/uploads/Overcoming-Animal-Phobias.pdf

Stress in Exotic animals https://millroadvet.co.nz/News-Stories/stress-in-exotic-animals

Exotic Animal Laws by State https://www.findlaw.com/injury/torts-and-personal-injuries/exotic-animal-laws-by-state.html

Detailed Discussion of the Exotic Pet Trade https://www.animallaw.info/article/detailed-discussion-exotic-pet-trade

The unregulated exotic pet trade in the EU: a threat to... https://www.eurogroupforanimals.org/news/unregulated-exotic-pet-trade-eu-threat-health-and-biodiversity

Species Conservation Industry Trends https://mazuri.com/blogs/partner-highlights/species-conservation-industry-trends?srsltid=AfmBOopm5uLCdpLfmFujkOvVpVjSFbxyP4vjqFHFWMniLouCB1fp_2-n

Our Reptile Forum https://ourreptileforum.com/community/

Pets groups https://www.meetup.com/topics/pets-animals/

Advocating for Meaningful Animal Welfare Policies ... https://www.aspcapro.org/resource/advocating-meaningful-animal-welfare-policies-through-storytelling

Exotic Animal Care https://theanimalcare.org/course/exotic-animal-care/

How to Build a Bioactive Terrarium for Your Reptile https://reptifiles.com/how-to-build-bioactive-terrarium/

Decoding Symbols: The Meaning of Parrots in Various ... https://medium.com/@levergreen/decoding-symbols-the-meaning-of-parrots-in-various-traditions-d8e6969ccf7b

Capturing the Wild at Home: Exotic Pet Photography Tips https://mysafarilove.com/guides/capturing-the-wild-at-home-exotic-pet-photography-tips/

How to Practice Mindfulness to Help You & Your Pets https://michaelrburke.com/how-practicing-mindfulness-will-help-you-your-pets/

Leave a Review

Thank You for Exploring the World of Exotic Pets with Us!

We hope you enjoyed reading **"Essential Guide to Exotic Pets"** and found it valuable for enhancing your pet-keeping journey. Your feedback means the world to us!

If the book helped you make informed decisions, offered helpful tips, or inspired you to care for your exotic pet differently, we would love to hear your thoughts. Leaving a review not only supports the author but also helps other pet enthusiasts discover this helpful resource.

Please take a moment to share your experience—whether it's your favorite tip, something new you learned, or how the guide made a difference in your pet care routine. Your honest review has a tremendous impact!

Thank you once again for being part of the exotic pet community. Your passion and support keep us going!

140

Free Handouts

Worksheets, trackers, checklists

Meet My Pet: Journal

https://docs.google.com/document/d/1QwGH4vKMCm7N24HxlJ8vEt8Dn11YU0PJs4ICsvk6om0/edit?usp=sharing

Nutrition Guide

https://docs.google.com/document/d/1ufn4K_wruh_BklV75KVnx2-3mno56TCsbaY4U7U_Ajc/edit?usp=sharing

Photoshoot Tips

https://docs.google.com/document/d/1TiUh4xm25UBnEAZX0MQFo4tPCgsckJkHiGUARBm_2To/edit?usp=sharing

www.ingramcontent.com/pod-product-compliance
Lightning Source LLC
Chambersburg PA
CBHW031420120626
46545CB00006B/2198